Restoration

BARRON'S

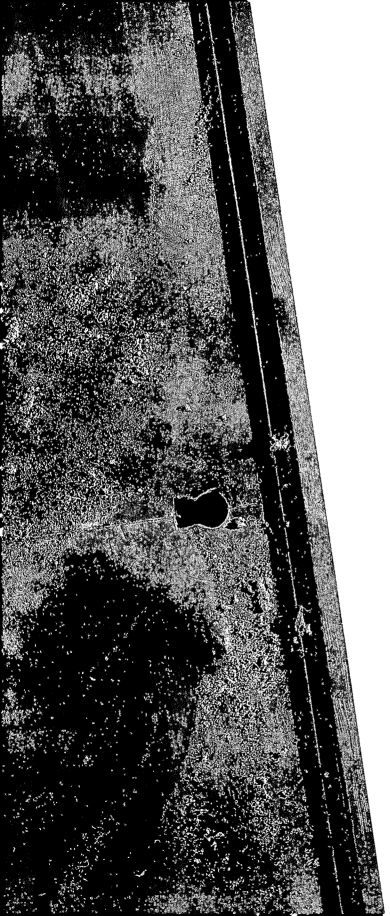

Original title of the book in Spanish: *Restauración*
© Parramon Ediciones, S.A., 1999. World Rights
Published by Parramon Ediciones, S.A., Barcelona, Spain

Text: Vicenc Gibert and Josep López
Step-by-step: Eduard Vall-Llosera
Series design: Carlos Bonet
Photography: Nos & Soto

Translated from the Spanish by Michael Brunelle
and Beatriz Cortabarria

All inquiries should be addressed to:
Barron's Educational Series, Inc.
250 Wireless Blvd.
Hauppauge, NY 11788
http://www.barronseduc.com

Library of Congress Catalog Card No.: 00-101638
International Standard Book No. 0-7641-5246-7

Printed in Spain

987654321

CONTENTS

INTRODUCTION

The trade of furniture restoration became popular at a time when society realized that an old piece of quality furniture was preferable to a new piece of furniture that was mass produced in a factory. It is difficult to pinpoint the origins of the furniture restoration profession because fine woodworkers have always repaired furniture that was broken and worn from use and the passage of time. Society was changed when it became possible to buy inexpensive furniture, thanks to mechanization and factories that specialized in making a few standardized designs. A consumer culture based on disposable objects was born, where it is more practical to buy new furniture rather than the traditional culture of conserving and restoring. This fact provoked the disappearance of many fine woodworkers and many other traditional trades of the sector, whose professionals abandoned their workshops, in many cases family owned, to work in factories; and this is how the role of the furniture restorer was relegated to the work of very few collectors of very specific pieces.

A good restorer has a mastery of the majority of the crafts related to the handling and the transformation of wood; he or she must be an expert woodworker, must know the profession of fine cabinetmaking to perfection, must have some knowledge of wood turning, marquetry, carving and, of course, must have a good command of the techniques characteristic of furniture restoration.

The most important role performed by the restorer is that of conservation, that is, to prevent the effects of the passage of time and the typical wear and tear from continuous use of the piece. If this preventative action is not possible, an alternate plan must be made to restore the qualities of the piece of furniture.

The interventions in a piece of furniture must be kept to a minimum in order for the piece to maintain as many original parts as possible. On this front, there are two different schools of thought: those who defend the position of a visible restoration, where one can see the areas that have been restored; and those who favor restorations that imitate the exact form of the original piece. Both possibilities are equally valid depending on the circumstances, but a repair job that goes well with the overall feeling of the piece of furniture is always preferable to a poor imitation.

This book is a compilation of the vast knowledge of an accomplished restorer whose mastery is based on the command of the trades of woodworking and fine cabinetmaking.

In the introduction, you will find information about the most common materials and tools, as well as the first steps to follow from the moment the decision is made to restore a piece of furniture. Demonstrated in the projects are some of the most frequent restoration jobs; they will serve as a guide and model of the majority of the projects whose objective is to transform wood furniture.

Finally, I would like to thank furniture restorers for the valuable job they perform, and with their sensibility, knowledge, respect and anonymity, make their work unnoticeable, so we may continue enjoying the most beautiful works of art.

Vicenç Gibert i Armengol

THE CRAFT OF THE RESTORER

The history of furniture and that of mankind are parallel. Furniture has been regarded for many years as very appreciated objects that are generally created for people with certain financial status. Until relatively recently, the old furniture pieces of great beauty and quality were not as popular as they are nowadays. This fact has favored the conservation and reuse of certain pieces of furniture, thus reviving the profession of furniture restoration.

It is understood that the older the piece of furniture, the greater the attention and the mastery the restorer must have. The various historical periods have created different furniture styles: the medieval period generated the Romanesque and Gothic; later, the Renaissance; the 17th century, the Baroque; the 18th century, the Rococo and the Neoclassic; and the 19th century, Modernism.

For a piece of furniture to be considered an antique, it must be more than 100 years old, but it must also have the characteristics of a good piece of furniture—that is, it must be made of fine woods or of certain quality, it must have been created by a good cabinetmaker, and if possible, it must have a particular trait such as carvings, marquetry, or a good design of a well-defined style.

The pieces of furniture that arrive at the restorer's shop are usually the common ones found at home—chests of drawers, tables, beds, chairs, armchairs, and so on. However, chairs, because of their continuous use, are most commonly repaired.

Most of the artisans who practice furniture restoration are fine cabinetmakers, who have good knowledge of the methods of working with wood and are highly skilled in the use of the tools common in carpentry. Nowadays, the restoration and repair of antique furniture is considered a specialized profession. Consequently, several schools have come into being, most of them led by master craftsmen specializing in the teaching of antique furniture restoration.

The restorer must be conscious of the fact that besides knowing how to build furniture, one must know the different types of joints, veneers, and finishes that exist, because in the normal practice of the trade, one will meet multiple problems related to these things.

In any furniture restoration, one of the main objectives is that the restoration be unnoticeable—that is, no matter what the repair is, it should be as discrete as possible. For example, any inlays, carvings, or moldings that have been lost should be made to match by the restorer. The same is true of the many pieces of hardware that are part of the furniture. Such items as the hinges, knobs, locks, and keyholes must match the original and can be purchased in specialized hardware stores.

Another problem that restorers face is that sometimes wood furniture is infested with wood-boring insects. Therefore, it has to be cleaned and treated to prevent such attacks in the future; to achieve this, special insecticides are used. In restoration, the idea that all the damaged and old wood must be removed is invalid, because in many cases this would eliminate nearly the entire piece.

Definitely, restoration is a profession that requires, among other qualities, great patience. Each restoration is different, and most of the time, if the furniture is being seen for the first time, the alterations should be unnoticeable, because, as we said before, for the restoration to be perfect it must be invisible or semi-invisible. Through restoration, the practical or decorative function of the furniture is returned, when before it was considered a piece of junk and always ended up in a corner or was discarded.

One of the most delicate steps that a good restorer must perform is the analysis of the furniture that comes to the shop, which is to say, how to evaluate the damage, what type of wood the furniture is made of, how the structure is designed, what kind of damage exists, and most important, if the furniture is worth restoring. If it is, the restorer must also consider how much intervention is required and which parts can be replaced.

1. The restorer's first task is to evaluate the furniture to see whether it is worth restoring. This chest of drawers, which is about 140 years old, is still decorative and usable despite the passage of time. Therefore, it is worth restoring.

2. A good restorer must know how to identify and evaluate the damage of the furniture, to determine the proper process for restoration. A preliminary inspection of this table reveals signs of infestation by wood-boring insects; small veneer pieces missing, especially on the tabletop; and damage to the side crosspiece. The strength of the table is unaffected, therefore it is unnecessary to replace the damaged crosspiece; it will be sufficient to repair the part.

3. Restored slant top desk with some extraordinary marquetry work on the front cover, which notably embellishes the entire piece. The restoration work must respect the original aesthetic and should never be inferior to the quality of the furniture.

4. Chairs often need to be restored as a result of continuous use. The seat is usually damaged and the legs loosened. Occasionally, the restorer must count on the collaboration of specialists to adequately restore the piece. In this case, the help of an upholsterer will be required to repair the damaged upholstery of the chair.

5. A bureau, obviously the fine work of a good cabinetmaker, with a marble top and carved decorations. The restorer, as much as possible, must preserve the original accessory elements, such as the marble, drawer pulls, keyholes, and mirrors.

6. Catalan dresser from the 18th century, before restoration. It is constructed of solid walnut, decorated with boxwood strip inlay and still displays the original hardware. The identification of the period when the piece was made will give the restorer useful information about the construction, decorative accessories, and types of ideal finishes.

7. The same dresser after restoration. Following repairs and restoration of the numerous cracks in the wood, the missing material, unglued parts, and the boxwood inlay in some areas, a natural finish has been applied, which corresponds to the style of the period of the piece.

MATERIALS AND PRODUCTS

It is difficult to mention each and every one of the materials and products used in furniture restoration. Therefore, in this chapter the most commonly used and most necessary will be presented, organized in the following manner: the wood, as the basic material for the job; the products used to clean the furniture and its components; the insecticides used to eliminate the wood-boring insects that could live inside the wood; glues, waxes, and fillers used to make minor repairs; the products used to bleach the wood; the stains used to color it; the materials used to finish it; and, finally, the hardware.

The wood. There are many kinds and species of trees and bushes whose wood is used. When a piece of furniture has to be restored, one of the first steps is to identify the wood, that way the restoration can be carried out with the same type of wood.

Sometimes, the required type of wood is no longer produced or is difficult to find. In these cases, the restorer uses the wood that best adapts to the needs and characteristics of the parts that have to be replaced.

Cleaning products. The basic products used to clean the furniture and its various components are ammonia diluted in water, strippers, alcohol, mineral spirits, turpentine, caustic soda, and window and metal cleaners.

Insecticides. The products used to eliminate wood-boring insects are liquids that must be applied with a syringe into the

holes left in the wood by the insects themselves. Aerosols, which can be applied to the surface, are also available.

Glues. The most commonly used glue in restoration is white glue, or polyvinyl acetate, which is water soluble. It is used for all types of restoration, and the drying time for a good bond is 24 hours. To hold small parts quickly, cyanocrilatic adhesives are normally used. Contact cement is used only for very short-term jobs because it loses its effectiveness with heat and humidity. There is also animal glue, made with animal bones, which is prepared in a double boiler. It is very effective, especially for gluing veneer.

1. Samples of the most commonly used woods in antique furniture: boxwood (A), walnut (B), ebony (C), mahogany (D), and oak (E).

2. To completely eliminate insect infestation in the wood, it is necessary to inject an insecticide product in the holes left by the wood-boring insect.

3. Contact cement, white glue (polyvinyl acetate or carpenter's glue) and a two-part epoxy glue.

4. Rabbit skin glue (animal glue) in sheet and granule forms.

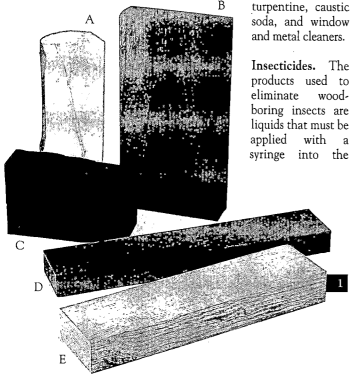

Waxes and fillers. Small areas of damage in wood can be repaired by applying waxes and fillers. The missing parts could be a result of breaks, the aging of the wood, dents, or wood-boring insects. In any case, tones similar to those of the wood to be restored can be always found.

Bleaching products. There are acids on the market for bleaching the wood and eliminating the possible traces of paint or stains accumulated in the pores. Most are mixed with water. Products like concentrated hydrogen peroxide solutions mixed with water or oxalic acid crystals dissolved in hot water can also be used.

Stains. After stripping wood, stains may appear, different colors between some woods and others may become apparent, and differences caused by aging may become evident. To unify the color of the wood, application of stains is recommended. Powdered dyes, like synthetic anilines, are soluble in both water and alcohol. There are also oil-based stains.

Finishing products. When we talk about finishes we are referring to the final look of the piece of furniture. In order to achieve a good finish, we can apply waxes that have been dissolved in turpentine; pure beeswax can also be purchased, and various products can be added to it to add hardness, color, scent, and glossiness.

The most commonly used varnishes for finishing furniture are nitrocellulose products, which fill the pores, and when dried are not too hard. They can be dissolved with mineral spirits. The polyurethane varnish creates a harder surface. Shellac is a varnish that is soluble in alcohol; when shellac dries, it leaves a hard and glossy surface.

Hardware. It is very useful to find a hardware store that specializes in hardware for wood furniture. Hardware can be made of various materials—such as iron, brass, or copper—and it can be galvanized, chromed, nickel plated, or brass plated. Many times, when the doors are taken off and the locks removed, the keyholes break and have to be replaced.

5. Waxes in bar form of various colors, colored fillers in tubes, and different coloring agents for making fillers in the workshop.

6. To bleach the wood, one of the available commercial products or oxalic acid crystals dissolved in hot water may be used.

7. Natural stains in powder form in rectangular dishes and synthetic aniline dyes that are soluble in water and alcohol.

8. A piece of beeswax, dissolved wax, bottle with synthetic polyurethane varnish, a darker bottle with shellac dissolved in alcohol, shellac in flake form, varnish for metals, and in the middle, bottles with alcohol and turpentine.

9. Hinge, piano hinge, bolts, knobs, handles, locks, and keyholes.

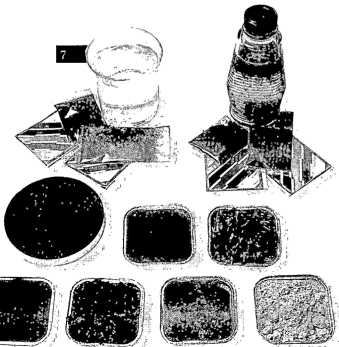

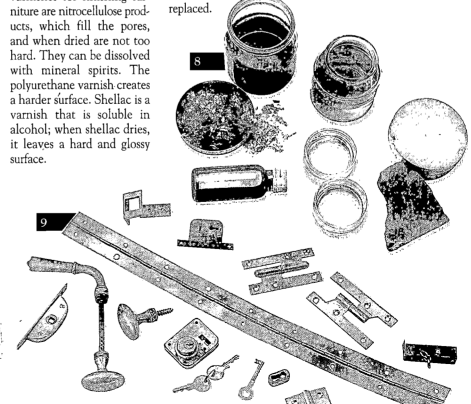

COMMONLY USED TOOLS

The tools used in the restoration of furniture are as varied as the ones used in woodworking. Many restorers make their own tools with simple materials. This is the case of the steel C-spring used to hold and clamp the wood.

In addition to a workbench, on which tasks can be carried out comfortably and a table that is sufficiently large, the tools that are indicated below are also needed.

Measuring and marking tools. The basic tools for these chores are a fine-point pencil of a medium hardness to mark in detail, a measuring tape, a carpenter's square, a sliding bevel square, a marking gauge to make parallel lines, and a com-

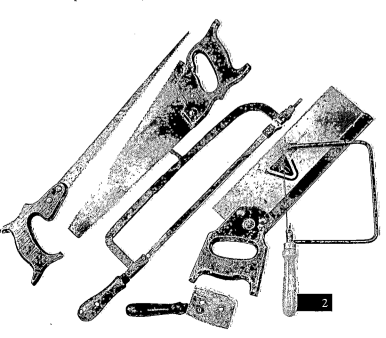

pass, which can be used to make curved lines and measure distances.

Sawing tools. In restoration projects, various handsaws are used. The most commonly used handsaw to repair furniture is the tenon saw, which allows the restorer to make very fine cuts. Also necessary are a veneer saw, which consists of a blade with teeth on both sides that can be used to cut off dowels; a hacksaw for metals; and a coping saw to do fretwork.

Fixed-blade cutting tools. They are used to plane and smooth the wood. Wooden ones are lighter than metal ones. In restoration, Japanese planes made of a wooden prism in which a blade is held by a wedge are used the most.

Other cutting tools. These are used for cutting mortises,

doing carvings, and removing material. In this section we must include chisels, mortise chisels, and gouges. The chisels have a beveled blade of different thicknesses, between ⅛ and 1⅝ inches (3 and 42 mm). Mortise chisels have a straight blade and a variable width between ³⁄₃₂ and ¾ inches (3 and 19 mm); they are used for making holes in the wood. Finally, the gouges are similar to the chisels but with a curved blade.

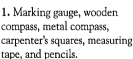

1. Marking gauge, wooden compass, metal compass, carpenter's squares, measuring tape, and pencils.

2. Point handsaw, regular handsaw, metal hacksaw, tenon saw, veneer saw, fretsaw.

3. Japanese smoothing planes.

4. A sampling of different chisels, gouges, and mortise chisels.

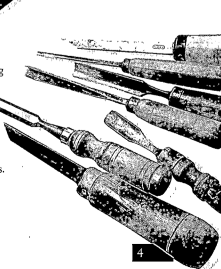

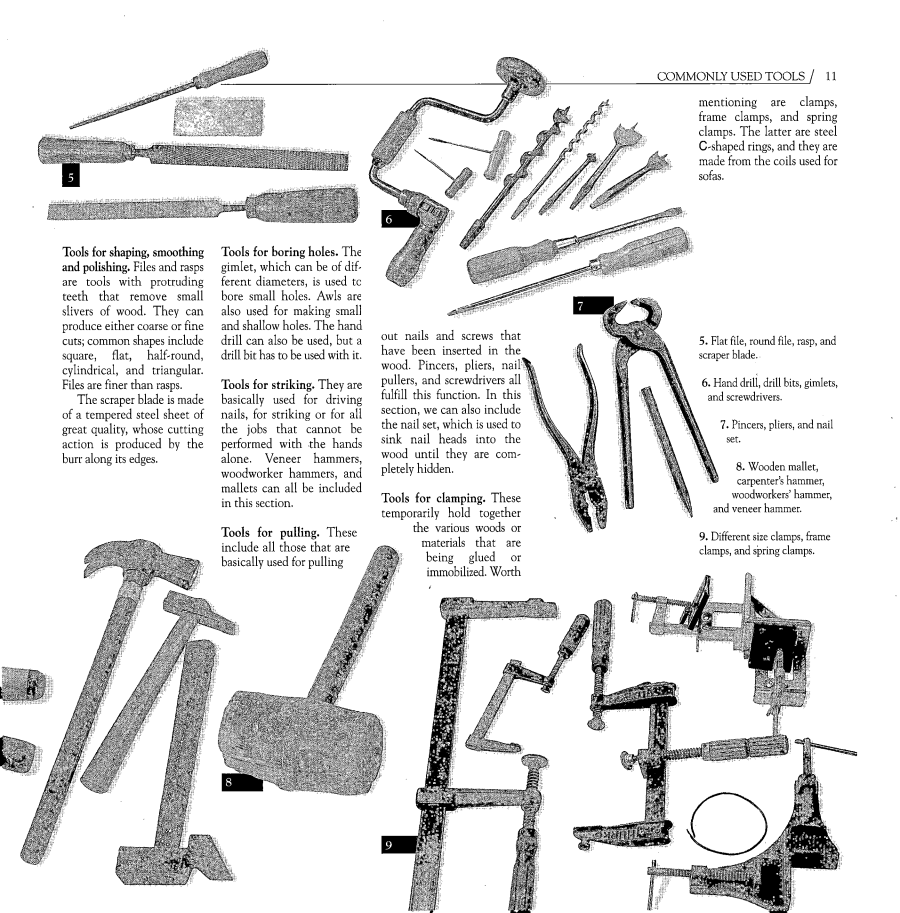

mentioning are clamps, frame clamps, and spring clamps. The latter are steel C-shaped rings, and they are made from the coils used for sofas.

Tools for shaping, smoothing and polishing. Files and rasps are tools with protruding teeth that remove small slivers of wood. They can produce either coarse or fine cuts; common shapes include square, flat, half-round, cylindrical, and triangular. Files are finer than rasps.

The scraper blade is made of a tempered steel sheet of great quality, whose cutting action is produced by the burr along its edges.

Tools for boring holes. The gimlet, which can be of different diameters, is used to bore small holes. Awls are also used for making small and shallow holes. The hand drill can also be used, but a drill bit has to be used with it.

Tools for striking. They are basically used for driving nails, for striking or for all the jobs that cannot be performed with the hands alone. Veneer hammers, woodworker hammers, and mallets can all be included in this section.

Tools for pulling. These include all those that are basically used for pulling out nails and screws that have been inserted in the wood. Pincers, pliers, nail pullers, and screwdrivers all fulfill this function. In this section, we can also include the nail set, which is used to sink nail heads into the wood until they are completely hidden.

Tools for clamping. These temporarily hold together the various woods or materials that are being glued or immobilized. Worth

5. Flat file, round file, rasp, and scraper blade.

6. Hand drill, drill bits, gimlets, and screwdrivers.

7. Pincers, pliers, and nail set.

8. Wooden mallet, carpenter's hammer, woodworkers' hammer, and veneer hammer.

9. Different size clamps, frame clamps, and spring clamps.

EVALUATION OF THE DAMAGE

When we talk about restoration we are always referring to the furniture itself, but the professional is a fundamental part of the process. The person who works in restoration must have a command of a series of techniques and disciplines in carpentry, fine woodworking, carving, marquetry, and so on, which will allow him to understand the piece of furniture that needs the work and to evaluate it properly so that the project can be carried out successfully.

Every restorer will apply techniques from other trades, but without a doubt, the restorer must also know the techniques of the trade, such as treating the piece for different wood-boring insects, including how to identify them and the degree of damage that they may represent. The restorer must also know how to clean the wood in order to return it to its original state and have some skill in adding and replacing parts and applying filler to damaged areas. Finally, the restorer must also know the secrets of a good finish in order to apply a stain or a varnish and to make the result homogeneous.

Visual examination
When a piece of furniture arrives at the restorer's shop with several imperfections, one of the first steps is a visual and general examination of the piece to evaluate all the damage. To that end, it is necessary to examine it from all angles, if possible, turning it and removing the different components (drawers, shelves, and so on) and opening all the doors.

The most common problems in wood furniture are broken parts; an unglued structure; broken and unglued decorative parts, veneers, and appliqués; damage of finishes; scratched, worn out, and soiled varnishes; damage from wood-boring insects and humidity; and loss of decorative elements, hardware, keyholes, escutcheons, keys, knobs, locks, and so on.

Determining how far a restoration should go or whether a partial or total replacement is better depends fundamentally on the degree of experience of the master restorer.

As in all other trades, there is a series of tasks that, depending on the type of furniture or on the part that needs to be restored, must be kept in mind. For example, in the case of chairs, one must pay special attention to the joints because the gluing of its pieces and the condition of the legs determine its strength. On the other hand, dressers usually suffer from loose joints in their frame and misalignments of the boards and the drawers because of sudden changes in humidity. For armoires in general, the structure should be evaluated and the adjustment of doors and the hardware—such as locks, keyholes, handles, keys, and hinges—checked.

When the structure of the piece is not loose, there is no need to disassemble it. Complete disassembly is a very expensive and elaborate task. Besides separating the parts and gluing them back, the old and dried out glue must be removed from the joints.

When some parts of the furniture have become loose, they can be repaired without having to take them apart completely, thus avoiding the disassembly of the entire piece. After gluing back the loose parts, repairs to those parts that are not part of the structure are done. Glue should be applied to the interior of the joint, taking special care not to loosen the other joints.

If through time the furniture has been subject to various poorly made repairs, the restorer should improve them applying his or her knowledge and criteria.

If it is necessary to disassemble the piece completely, it is very useful to first number the various parts, to make the reassembly easier later.

The furniture should not be struck directly with a hammer or a mallet when taking it apart because the joints could be damaged or the parts could break. In cases like these, a piece of wood is placed over the part so that wood receives the impact of the hammer or mallet.

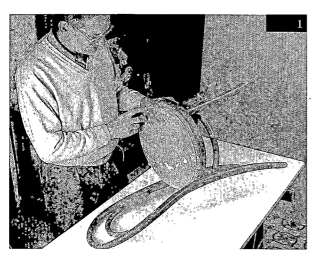

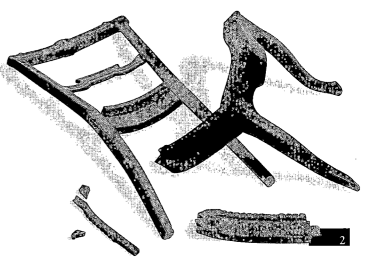

1. The first thing a restorer should do is carry out a detailed examination of the furniture to determine the most appropriate restoration process. Notice how in this case the master restorer carefully analyzes the condition of a chair.

2. All of the parts that make up the frame of this chair have come unglued, and the caned web that constituted the seat has completely disappeared.

3. The dresser suffers from misalignments in its frame, drawers, and boards because of rapid changes in humidity. There are also pieces of veneer missing and the legs are worn out. The dresser is dirty and it also has stains and damaged varnish as a result of aging.

4. This walnut bookcase is broken and has lost pieces in the lower area of one of the sides from wood-boring insects. The sidepiece and the lost leg must be replaced.

5. The condition of the inside of the wood, which has suffered insect attack, is tested with the help of an awl.

6. The lower parts of the piece of furniture have been damaged by humidity, and some veneer has broken off.

7. Joints have broken because of rot and insect attack. In this case, the lateral crosspiece must be replaced with a new one because this is an important structural piece.

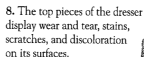

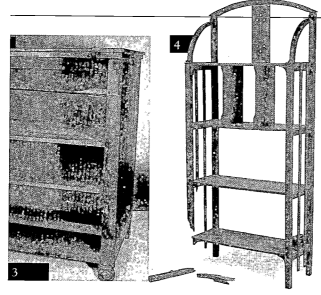

8. The top pieces of the dresser display wear and tear, stains, scratches, and discoloration on its surfaces.

9. On one of the sides of the piece of furniture, a piece of mahogany veneer has broken off.

10. Sometimes we are faced with pieces of furniture that have been subject to poorly done repairs, such as this chair, which displays a repair that lacks aesthetic value.

11. The evaluation of the decorative elements of this trunk reveals a handle missing and damage on the other one; also, the outside surface of the trunk was covered with fabric held in place with nails. Because it is impossible to repair the original fabric and handle, they must be eliminated.

12. Sometimes, it is absolutely necessary to take apart a piece of furniture completely to be able to restore it properly. Such is the case of this Thonet style rocker made of stained beech.

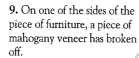
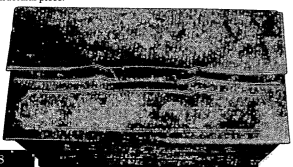
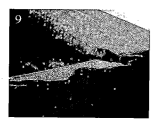

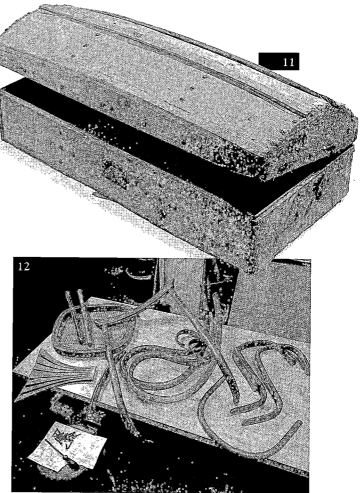

PRESERVATION

Preserving a piece of furniture involves cleaning the exterior and the interior of the wood. For the exterior, products that are quite abrasive are generally used; therefore, they must be used with care so as not to damage the wood. The interior cleaning must be considered a curative process, because some woods are infested with wood-boring insects, which produce a series of perforations that damage the wood structurally and aesthetically.

Light, temperature, and humidity also affect the condition of the wood. Excess humidity produces much of the physical damage in the wood.

Wood-Boring Insects

Generally, the insects that infest wood are known as wood-boring, or wood eating, insects. The wood-boring beetle, moths, and termites are examples.

Some woods are more prone to infestation than others. For example olive, walnut, and oak are especially sensitive to wood-boring insects. On the other hand, mahogany is immune to insects.

In wood infestations, the female lays her eggs in the crevices and the loose joints. The larvae that emerge are very small, and they consume the inside of the wood

for two years, during which time the cycle repeats itself and the female keeps spreading the eggs throughout the piece of furniture. After the two years, the wood-boring insects surface, and they transform into beetles with wings. This is, in short, the repetitive life cycle of wood-boring insects.

The beetle emerges toward the end of spring or at the beginning of summer. At these times one must pay close attention to furniture pieces. Wood-boring insects are detected, thanks to the piles of yellow sawdust found under the furniture or near it.

When these piles of sawdust are noticed, the furniture must be examined to discover the beetles' exit holes. Following that, an insecticide must be applied, sprayed, brushed, or injected or the furniture must be immersed in it.

The most recommended technique is to inject the insecticide with a syringe into all the holes found and to soak the remaining surface with a small brush. The insecticide can also be sprayed on, using the product in aerosol form. The application must be carried out in a well-ventilated place, using gloves and a mask.

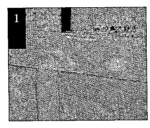

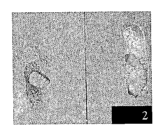

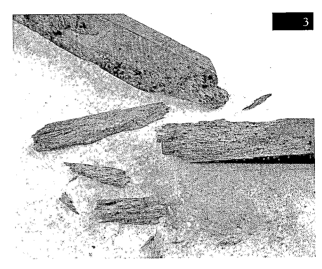

1. The back side of this bureau shows infestation by wood-boring insects.

2. Observe the two wood-boring insects inside of the wood.

3. The wood-boring beetle lays its eggs in the crevices and cracks of the wood. The larva lives in it and is nourished by it, making round holes. Its presence is detected through the small sawdust piles found around the furniture.

4. An insecticide must be injected in all the holes and brushed over the entire surface, to eliminate the insects that have attacked the wood.

5. After the insecticide has been applied, it is recommended that the wood be put inside a plastic bag, closed as tightly as possible, for 24 hours. This operation is repeated after 15 days.

6. The insecticide can also be sprayed onto the surfaces of the parts with an aerosol form of the product.

7. Once the final finish has been applied to the furniture, the small holes produced by the wood-boring insects can be covered with a hard wax. The wax is rolled with the fingers and inserted in the holes with a wooden spatula.

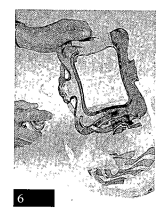

6

7

Humidity and temperature

Wood, like all organic materials, is hygroscopic—that is, its relative humidity tends to maintain a balance in relation to the humidity of the surroundings. When the wood contains about 20% humidity, it is exposed to fungi attack, and at 30% humidity, it is the optimum medium. Depending on the type of fungi, the attack can stain the wood or destroy the walls of the cells that form it.

The air always contains a certain quantity of water vapor, which will vary according to the temperature. The higher the temperature, the higher the capacity to absorb water (humidity).

All organic materials contain humidity in a higher or lower quantity. If the humidity of the surroundings is higher than that of the material, the furniture tends to absorb the humidity from the surroundings; if on the other hand, the humidity of the surroundings is less than that of the furniture, it tends to release it.

Because of this, one must keep in mind that changes in humidity and temperature alter the wood, and the greater its surface and the smaller its thickness the more rapidly it reacts to changes in humidity.

Humidity must be considered an aggressive agent, attacking not only wood but also other materials of which the furniture is made. In general, furniture is made of wood elements bonded with glue, which can be altered in a humid environment. So special attention should be given to veneer pieces that become unglued from the furniture as a result of humidity. In these cases, it is desirable to make the repair in a relatively short time, or there is a risk that the entire veneer will be damaged.

8. Samples of various woods infested by wood-boring insects and woods that have rotted as a result of humidity.

9. Because of excessive humidity, the veneer has come off of the furniture. Wood reacts more rapidly to changes in humidity when the surface is large and the thickness is small.

10. Wood attacked by fungi, one of wood's most dangerous enemies.

11. Other problems that affect wood are cracking and splitting, because wood contracts and expands, especially when it is exposed to changes in temperature and humidity.

8

9

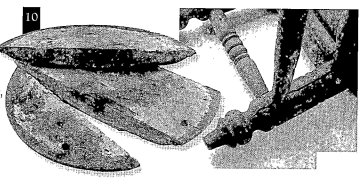

10

CLEANING AND STRIPPING

The first phase of restoration is the proper cleaning of the furniture. If the finish is not very damaged and it is not necessary to remove the layers of old paint or varnish, the elimination of grime and dirt will suffice. To do this, either warm water and a neutral soap or a solution of water and ammonia can be used.

When the wood has thick layers of damaged paint or varnish, or when the color of the piece is uneven from continuous use, the piece should undergo a stripping process.

Stripping is also used when the wood is of good quality and the restorer wishes to return it to its natural color and grain.

There are many stripping techniques. Here they are classified as either chemical or mechanical.

Chemical stripping

The chemical stripping techniques are based on the elimination of the layer of paint or varnish from the surface with chemicals that soften the varnish, which later must be removed. The most commonly used stripping products are alcohol, caustic soda, and stripping gel.

The type of products selected will depend on the type of wood, paint, or varnish that is to be eliminated and, above all, on the general condition of the furniture.

Alcohol
The use of alcohol as a stripping agent is highly recommended when the varnish has been applied with a rubbing pad. Also, because alcohol evaporates very quickly, it can be used on veneer and marquetry. Alcohol is not toxic to the touch and is inexpensive. It can be applied liberally with cheesecloth and, after the varnish has softened, it is removed with a clean rag.

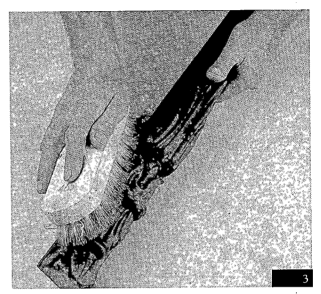

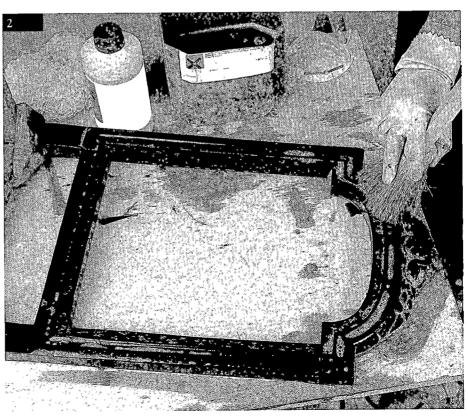

1. To remove the layer of grime and dust from the surface, the wood is washed with warm water and neutral soap, using a pad of 000 steel wool to dislodge the grime. It is rinsed with a wet cloth dipped in clean water and dried with a clean rag.

2. In moldings and pieces with reliefs, grime can be removed with a brush soaked in a solution of ammonia and water.

3. When the wood has carvings and other decorative motifs, it is advisable to use a brush to eliminate the dust.

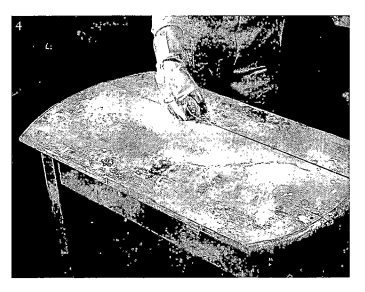

4. Caustic soda is applied with cotton rags: The rags are saturated in the caustic soda solution and are squeezed onto the surface to be stripped.

5. With the rags, the caustic soda solution is spread over the entire surface.

6. To remove the caustic soda, soak a cotton rag in clean water and, always following the grain of the wood, remove the caustic soda while rubbing the wood with a steel pad with the other hand. Continue with this procedure until the caustic soda is completely removed with clean water, changing cotton rags as often as needed.

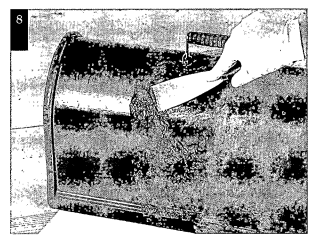

Caustic soda

Caustic soda, because of its corrosiveness, is used exclusively on solid pine. Before it is applied, it is diluted in water in a proportion of 2 pounds (1 kg) of caustic soda to 1 gallon (5 liters) of hot water, stirring until it is totally dissolved. Caustic soda should never be used on areas with veneer or marquetry because the water in the solution would soften the glue and cause the veneer and pieces of marquetry to come loose.

Caustic soda is applied with cotton rags soaked in the solution and squeezed over the wood until the wood is thoroughly soaked and the solution is spread evenly over the surface. Caustic soda is removed by rinsing the wood with tap water using cotton rags. The entire process must be carried out in a well-ventilated place and using long neoprene gloves, a mask, and safety glasses.

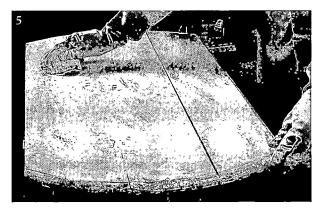

Chemical strippers

There are many types of chemical strippers on the market. They are applied over the wood with big or small brushes and they are left to work for about two minutes, depending on the type of varnish or paint that has to be removed. The layer of paint is loosened and removed with a spatula, and any remaining stripper is removed with cotton strands soaked in water or mineral spirits.

The use of neoprene gloves and a mask is required because chemical strippers are toxic and irritate the respiratory system.

7. To eliminate old paint, stripping gel is very practical. To apply, follow the manufacturer's directions carefully, protecting your hands with gloves and using a mask.

8. The stripping gel is left to work for a few minutes and, when the paint begins to crack, the paste formed by the gel and the old paint is removed with a spatula.

Mechanical stripping

In addition to using detergents and chemical strippers, restorers can clean wood through mechanical procedures, using different tools and products to eliminate the layers of paint and varnish, such as sanding, scraping, and hot air guns. Scraping can be used in conjunction with detergents and chemical strippers. Nevertheless, scraping is usually done on flat surfaces that are easy to polish.

Most pieces of old furniture have carvings and moldings that are very difficult to clean with scrapers.

For this, a brush with plastic or metal bristles is used so that all corners can be reached; also, universal solvent can be applied for a more effective cleaning.

9. For mechanical stripping different tools are needed, such as a torch, esparto, a rasp, and a brush with plastic or metal bristles.

10. To eliminate traces of paint from carvings and moldings, where it is difficult to use scrapers, cheesecloth soaked with mineral spirits can be used.

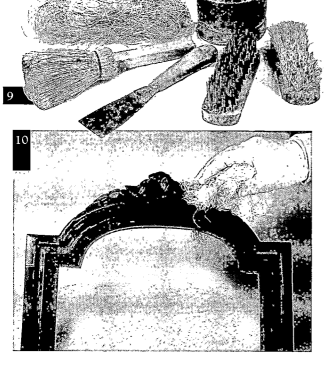

Sanding

Sanding is used not only to finish the piece, leaving the surface smooth and fine to the touch, but also to eliminate traces of varnish, grime, stains, and scratches during stripping. There is a great variety of sanding tools. Those used for wood are normally made of paper backing and their roughness varies from the coarsest grain of 40 to the finest 400 (see page 25). Nevertheless, for stripping purposes, the coarsest sandpapers are used—those of 40, 50, and 60 grits.

When the surfaces to be stripped are large and even, an electric portable belt sander is used. Belt sanders are available in different sizes, and the sandpaper belts come in corresponding sizes. Sandpaper can also be used directly on the surface, wrapped around a block of wood and rubbed vigorously.

11. There is a large variety of sandpapers for wood, from a grit of 40 (very coarse) to a grit of 400 (very fine). They also come in different formats, including sheets, roles, blocks, and discs.

12. For the mechanical sanding of large, even surfaces, an electric portable belt sander can be used, like the one shown in the illustration.

13. For manual sanding of large, even surfaces, a block of wood is covered with a sheet of fine sandpaper.

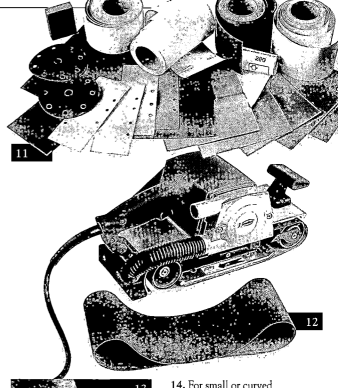

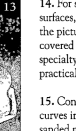

14. For small or curved surfaces, like the ones shown in the picture, sponge blocks covered with sandpaper sold in specialty stores are very practical.

15. Concave areas, like the curves in moldings, can be sanded manually by wrapping the sandpaper around the index finger.

Hot air gun

This is used for stripping solid wood with very thick layers of paint and varnish. It is ideal for large surfaces because it works fast and is easy to use. The paint softens and curls from the application of hot air, which allows its removal with a spatula.

19. The hot air gun heats the paint adhered to the wood.

20. When paint softens, it is removed with a spatula.

Scraping

This method is slower than manual sanding, but it is the best method for sanding shaped pieces that are solid wood such as legs and railing and that are in poor condition. Handled scrapers or blade scrapers of different shapes can be used.

16. Scraping produces a very fine and clean finish on the surface of the wood.

17. For solid wood furniture pieces that are shaped like these rounded bars, blade scraping is the most appropriate scraping method.

18. The handle scraper is used to completely eliminate the varnish in hard to reach areas and corners.

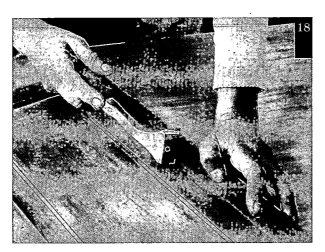

REPLACING AND REPAIRING PIECES

The processes for replacing parts or elements in a piece of furniture are determined by the knowledge of certain carpentry techniques and gluing methods: the replacement and substitution of structures and framework, the addition of new parts, the placement of parts of pieces, the addition and reparation of veneer and marquetry, and replacement of fillers.

Adding new parts

The addition of new parts to a piece of furniture is done keeping in mind the conservation of the entire piece. Framework should always be of the same type and quality as the wood from which the furniture is made.

In the repair of the structural elements of different types of furniture, it is often recommended to replace all of the parts that make it up, because the structure of the piece must be totally durable.

The elements of a piece of furniture that most commonly suffer damage are drawers, whose wear and tear from the constant rubbing is inevitable. The constant friction of a drawer causes considerable damage, especially when it is overloaded with more weight than it should have. Broken areas or those that are most worn should be repaired,

because a problem area always causes more damage.

In the same way, chairs also are frequently damaged because of improper and incorrect use. The legs, the chair back, and the joints of many stretchers are parts that require constant repair.

In addition to the new life that can be given to furniture from the repairs that are made, like adding new parts, the restorer must keep in mind the importance of maintaining and conserving the piece. For example, the lower parts of furniture can suffer damage

that requires a restorer to completely repair areas like the legs.

To properly add new parts to a piece of furniture, one must be completely familiar with the different woodworking techniques, and the use of the tools and knowledge of the processes of working with the material.

1. When a part of the framework of the furniture is very damaged, it is better to replace it with a new piece, as is the case of this table where the side crosspiece and the long crosspiece are in very bad shape. The side crosspiece is cut off flush with the leg.

2. To replace the crosspiece, the restorer cuts a piece of the same wood with the same dimensions as the one being replaced. Then, the location and size of the joint is measured and the mortise is cut. The piece is cut to the correct size so that it will fit into the legs properly.

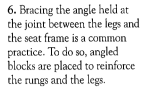

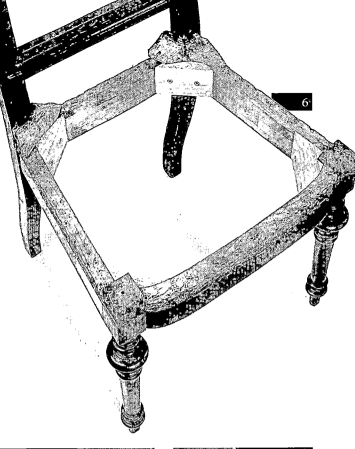

6. Bracing the angle held at the joint between the legs and the seat frame is a common practice. To do so, angled blocks are placed to reinforce the rungs and the legs.

7. The cane webbing of the chair seat and back are commonly damaged and must be replaced entirely.

8. Damage of the joint between the leg and frame is very common. In order to repair it, it must first be hollowed with a drill.

9. A new dowel is made and rounded using a plane.

10. The dowel is inserted into the leg, where glue has been previously applied. Then glue is applied to the inside of the support where the leg will be placed.

3. Following the same procedure the crosspiece is cut. A tenon is cut at each end with a chisel and a tenon saw, to fit into the lateral crosspiece.

4. The fit of the mortise and tenon and the fit between the new long crosspiece and the original lateral crosspiece is checked.

5. The new parts are glued in place with clamps.

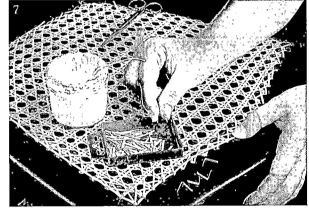

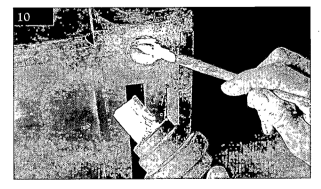

Replacing and repairing pieces

It is not always necessary to replace a piece in its entirety. On the contrary, in some antique pieces of furniture, it is preferable to maintain, as much as possible, the integrity of the original material of which the piece of furniture is made. But if this is impossible, small areas of the pieces should be replaced.

Sometimes, the joints of the chair's legs must be reinforced by inserting dowels with white glue in previously drilled holes. In some curved wood parts, it may be necessary to place a reinforcing piece into the structure itself.

In certain cases, it will be necessary to make moldings that are of the same shape as those of the furniture that is being restored. For this, profile templates can be used so the forms can be reproduced, or templates can simply be drawn from a piece that has already been removed.

Other parts that suffer considerable damage and wear and tear are marquetry work, veneers, and inlay. For these to be repaired properly, it is necessary to apply the techniques of the processes used to make the furniture. In the old days, veneers were bonded with rabbit skin glue that was prepared in a double boiler. Special attention must be given to the cutting and gluing of veneers and

marquetry because they are part of the decorative elements of the furniture, and the repairs will be visible.

Inlaid wood or other materials must also be treated with care, being sure to completely clean and repair the old areas and adding the necessary inlay afterward with white glue. Spring clamps are usually used to hold or clamp pieces with small dimensions in place.

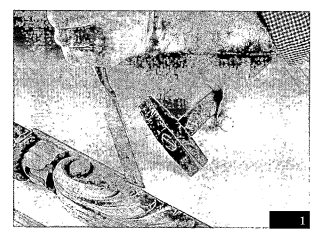

1. In this carved piece, a small damaged area must be replaced. The pieces of damaged wood that are going to be substituted, will be removed with a hammer and chisel. Notice that the new strips have been already prepared.

2. White, or polyvinyl acetate, glue is applied to the new pieces, and they are held in place with masking tape.

3. When the glue is dry, the excess wood of the new part is smoothed with a plane to match the existing piece.

4. To add a piece to the front part of the carved area, a notch is cut in the wood to help hold the new part in place.

5. The new piece is glued, fit into place, and clamped.

6. When the glue is dry, the piece is carved, beginning by removing material with the gouge. Notice how the piece is held in place by clamping it to the worktable, using a wooden block to avoid damaging the piece.

7. Various gouges and chisels are used to carve and shape the added piece.

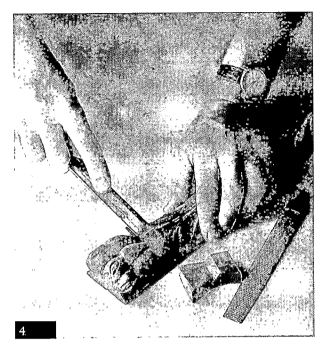

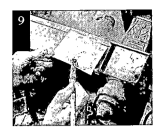

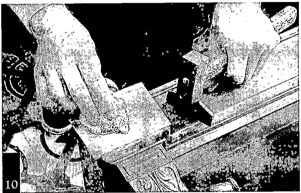

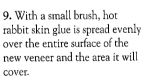

8. In order to replace a piece of veneer that is in bad shape, the sheet of veneer must first be completely removed using a chisel.

9. With a small brush, hot rabbit skin glue is spread evenly over the entire surface of the new veneer and the area it will cover.

10. The veneer is placed on the furniture and pressed with a veneer hammer. Then, pressure is applied to the entire glued surface with the hand and some cheesecloth.

11. Adding material to the inside of the frame of a seat. The wood blocks have been bonded with white glue and their fit adjusted with a chisel.

12. Here the wood pieces are bonded to the top crosspiece of a chair back. Note the way the clamps have been placed.

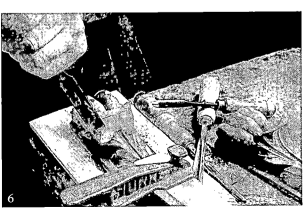

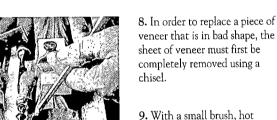

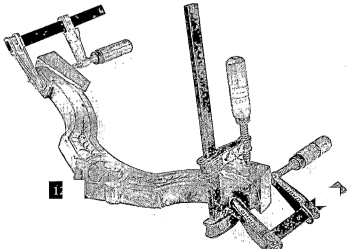

FILLING

The process of covering small imperfections in the wood is carried out using fillers. They are also used to fill small holes resulting from wood-boring insects. Small, superficial cracks can also be repaired with fillers.

There are commercially made fillers on the market that are as good as those made in the workshop; they contain cellulose and synthetic derivatives. Some can also be dyed to obtain the desired color. Regardless of the type used, fillers are applied over the imperfections with a spatula, smoothing them out over the surface of the wood and eliminating the excess.

All fillers shrink when they dry, so repair will require several applications and subsequent drying, until all the holes and crevices are perfectly filled. It is always necessary to do a final sanding, which will remove excess filler and blend it into the wood surface.

When it comes to the color of the filler, it is important to keep in mind that because of its composition, the varnish that will be applied over it will not stain it. It is preferable to prepare the fillers in a darker tone so once the piece of furniture is varnished, there will be no irregularity in the color.

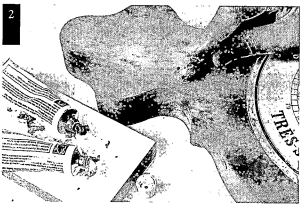

1. To eliminate the old filler, rub the surface with a cotton rag soaked in alcohol, and remove the old filler from the holes with the help of an awl.

2. Holes produced by wood-boring insects are filled with commercial fillers.

3. Sometimes the filler must be applied in the small interior crevices of carvings.

Hard waxes

In addition to fillers, mixtures of hard wax are also used to fill holes. These are applied after the wood has been finished, making it much simpler to choose the appropriate color.

Hard waxes are available in long bars and in different tones, and they can be mixed with each other. To prepare a mixture, a small piece is taken from the bars of each wax that the restorer wishes to mix and a hot air gun is used to melt them. When the wax cools off, it is kneaded with the fingers until a cylinder is formed. Then, the wax is applied over the holes with a wooden spatula. To obtain the desired tone, aniline dyes can be added to the dissolved wax, which makes it easy to obtain a large selection of colors.

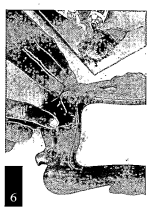

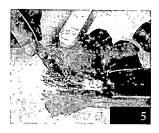

4. The process of heating the colored waxes with the help of a hot air gun.

5. Once the waxes have melted, they can be mixed together until a homogenous paste has formed.

6. Prepared fillers are applied with the help of a small spatula.

7. The filler can also be applied with a chisel.

SANDING

Sanding is a very important process in all tasks related to carpentry, because it helps to prepare the surface to receive the final finish, which will leave the surface smooth to the touch. Keep in mind that a good sanding will result in an excellent finish.

Sanding is always done in the direction of the grain of the wood, because if it is done against the grain, marks and scratches can be left on the wood that would be accentuated with the final finish.

There is a great variety of sandpaper of different qualities. Sandpaper is a strong paper with glass dust or sand on one of its sides, bonded with an adhesive product. The difference between the various types of sandpaper is the coarseness of its grit, which is specified with a system of numbers printed on the back of the paper. The differences in the quality and the coarseness of the sandpaper's grit enables the restorer to achieve various finishes and a very smooth surface. To begin the sanding process, coarse sandpaper is used, followed by a finer one for the finish. As can be seen in the table below, the coarsest grit corresponds to the number 40 and the finest to number 400:

40	very coarse
50	very coarse
60	coarse
80	coarse
100	medium
120	medium
150	fine
180	fine
240	very fine
280	very fine
320	very fine
400	very fine

Sandpaper can also be used by wrapping it around a wooden block with flat sides, one of which should be covered with a layer of cork, so as not to scratch the wood being sanded. This sanding block should have small enough dimensions that a person will be able to use it with a single hand.

An electric belt sander is used for large and flat surfaces. This is a machine that is made of lightweight materials and that holds a sandpaper belt that rotates at high speed.

All sanded surfaces require a final rubbing with a fine or extra fine steel wool pad to remove the marks left by the sandpaper and to adequately finish the surfaces for the final finish with wax or varnish. Instead of steel wool, fine-grit wet sandpaper can also be used for the sanding. Its numbering goes from 400 to 2,000. Before using this type of sandpaper, it is necessary to wet it in water, because it must always be wet when sanding.

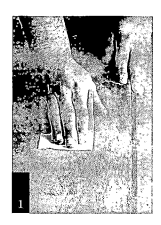

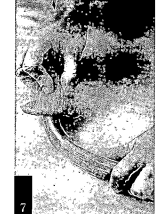

1. Sanding must always be done in the direction of the grain. Pressure is applied with the fingertips, not with the palm of the hand. Because many antique woods are irregular, varying the pressure applied with the fingertips allows the restorer to follow the surface properly.

2. It is easier to sand the flat edges of a board with a sanding block.

3. When dealing with a large surface and solid wood that is in good condition, it is faster to sand with an electric belt sander.

4. Sanding a molding while resting the index finger on the paper.

5. In this case, the sandpaper is pushed into the molding of the ring with the thumb.

6. Before the final finish, the wood must be sanded with 400-grit sandpaper, to achieve a surface that is completely flat and smooth to the touch.

7. After the sanding is done and before the wax is applied, it is necessary to rub the wood with a fine or extra fine steel wool pad to eliminate any marks that may have been left after sanding.

FINISHING

The finish that is applied to the wood in the final phase of a restoration gives the piece an aesthetic and technical quality that is required in a professional job.

A good finish, besides its aesthetic function, serves to protect the wood from external attacks. Therefore, applying a wax, a paint, a stain, or a varnish always serves the same purpose—to protect and embellish. Keep in mind that these protections do not affect in any way the structure of the wood.

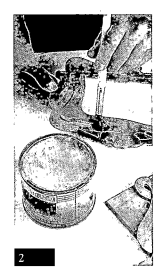

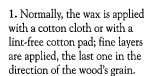

1. Normally, the wax is applied with a cotton cloth or with a lint-free cotton pad; fine layers are applied, the last one in the direction of the wood's grain.

2. It is better to use a more liquid wax and to apply it with a small brush to get into all of the grooves.

Waxes

Natural wax is one of the most common and oldest finishes. In restoration, the most appropriate is pure beeswax in paste form. However, there are commercially available waxes of different qualities, consistencies, and colors, already prepared and dissolved in turpentine, which can be applied directly on the wood.

The wax is applied to the surface of the wood with a cotton cloth or lint-free finishing pad or a small brush; once dry, it is buffed vigorously with a wool or cotton cloth to polish it.

There are also waxes in bar form with a wide variety of colors that adapt to any tone of the wood; they are used to cover imperfections, holes made by wood-boring insects, and minor flaws (see page 24).

Paint

The various types of paints on the market are classified according to their medium: oil paint, acrylic paint, and enamel paint. Oil paints are based on oils of plant origin, such as linseed oil, and they are diluted with mineral spirits or turpentine, which causes them to dry very slowly. They are used to paint over varnished or lacquered woods.

Acrylic paints have a water base and a matte finish, and they dry much faster. They must always be applied over clean wood, the grain filled and well sanded.

Enamel paints use oil-based varnishes and cellulose as a medium for application. They dry fast and the finish is glossy.

3. Enamel paint, which dries fast and has a glossy finish, is ideal for pieces that must be resistant to scratches and frequent use.

Stains

Stains are available in powder or liquid form.

There are three kinds of stains: water, alcohol, and oil based. The most popular stain used for restoration is walnut, which is usually oil based. Of course there is a wide variety of colors available on the market.

There is also a type of colored dyes called aniline dyes, which can be soluble in either water or alcohol. Both are applied with a brush, spread evenly over the entire surface to be stained.

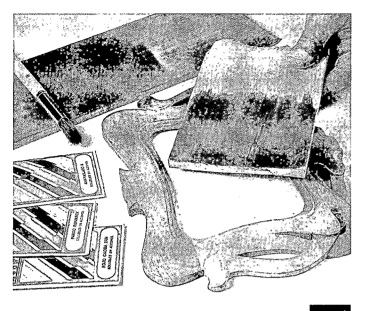

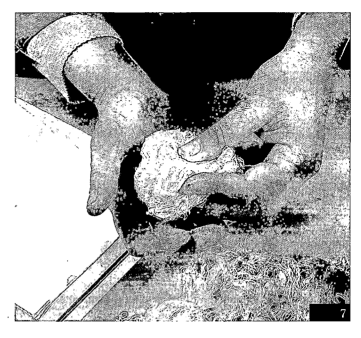

4

5

4. Wood is stained with synthetic aniline dyes. Before staining the furniture, it is advisable to run a test on a piece of old wood.

5. Carved wood is stained using a small brush to get into all of the hard to reach areas.

6. Once the finish has been applied to the furniture, it is retouched with an alcohol-based stain to hide the small added areas.

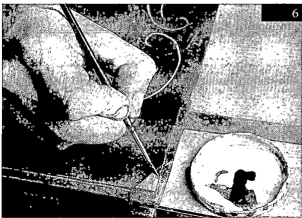

6

Varnishing with shellac

Another finish that is commonly used is varnish. This can be done with polyurethane varnish (see below) or with shellac, an older varnishing process that is also called lacquer. Some restorers prefer lacquering to varnishing with modern products.

Shellac is sold in flake form, which is obtained from insects that live in wood; there are some variations in color. Various types of shellac can be bought in liquid form and can be applied directly. Shellac can also be prepared in the workshop, quickly and easily by dissolving 8 ounces (200 g) of shellac flakes with 1 quart (1 liter) of alcohol, mixing them thoroughly until the flakes are completely dissolved.

The most commonly used method of applying shellac is with a finishing pad, which is made by gathering' clean, cotton strands or cheesecloth into a ball wrapped with a piece of cloth, also made of cotton.

Varnishing with polyurethane

This varnish produces a glossy, smooth surface and is best applied with cotton rags or with a small brush. After varnishing a piece of furniture with polyurethane, it is sanded and polished with steel wool. The final finish is achieved by applying wax with cotton

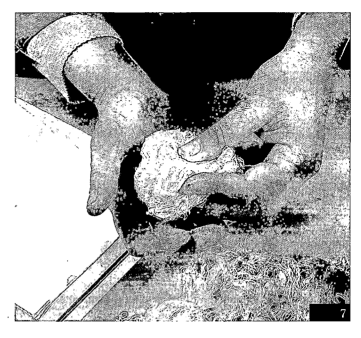

7

rags and then polishing with a clean cotton cloth.

7. Shellac is applied with a finishing pad. To form it, a clean cotton cloth and cotton strands or cheesecloth are required. A tight ball of strands the size of a fist is made; one side is pounded to create a flat, compressed surface.

8. The flat surface of the ball is covered with a square piece of cotton fabric so that it is perfectly centered. The four corners of the square are gathered at the top of the ball.

9. While holding the ball with one hand, the four corners are twisted tightly so that they stay together to form a handle.

10. To apply shellac, the handle of the pad must be held with the little finger and the ring finger against the palm of the hand; the thumb and index fingers are placed in a tripod shape to hold the sides of the pad.

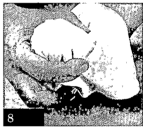

8

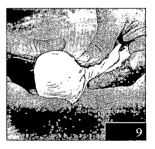

9

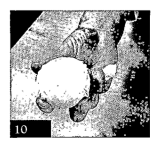

10

MODERNIST FRAME

W̌hen carrying out a restoration, besides making repairs on the object or piece of furniture, it is sometimes necessary to incorporate new pieces in order to improve the use of the restored piece. This is the case in the following project, which consists of a modernist frame, where besides making repairs, we have added a supporting stand on the back.

1. The poor state of the satinwood frame before restoration.

2. The project begins with an evaluation of the frame's damage. The first analysis shows that, besides repairing some loose parts, it is necessary to reconstruct one of them.

3. If the frame is turned over, the inset can be seen as can several holes that wood-boring insects have produced.

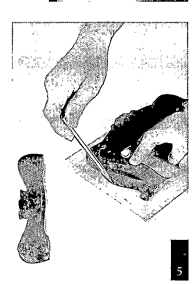

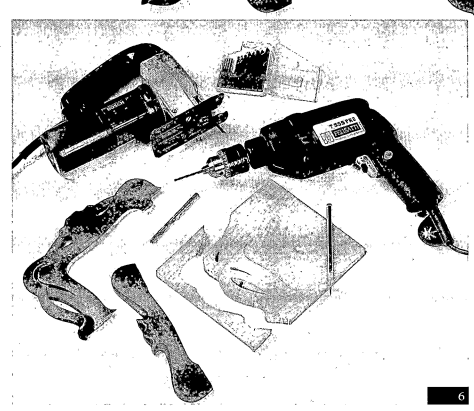

4. Detail of the wood damage that the wood-boring insects caused.

5. The first step in the restoration consists of making a copy of the outline of the part to be remade on a piece of wood of the same color, if possible. To do this, the part that is not damaged can be used as a pattern. For this project, cherry wood is used because it is similar to satinwood.

6. The outline of the part is cut out with a jigsaw. To cut the inside shapes, a hole is made with a drill so that the saw blade can be inserted to comfortably cut out the shapes.

7. Once the entire part is cut out, the frame is put together after trimming the excess wood from the sides; then it is glued with white glue.

8. To guarantee that all the individual parts bond properly, the pieces are held together with spring clamps. The excess glue from the joints is wiped off with a cloth dampened in water.

9. Because the frame is infested with wood-boring insects an insecticide is injected into all the holes of the piece.

10. It is also recommended to spray the outside with an aerosol insecticide and to put the frame into a plastic bag, seal it well and leave it for 10 to 15 days.

11. After the frame is rid of the insects, the carving can begin. To do this, the frame is tightly held in place on the workbench with an additional piece of wood and a clamp; then the design is carved with a v-groover and a hammer.

12. With the wood still in place, the molding is shaped with a curved gouge, following the pattern and style of the frame.

13. The pores and small imperfections are covered with filler, which is applied with a spatula. The filler must be of the same tone as the wood. To do this, commercially prepared fillers are mixed until the desired color is obtained.

14. In order to ensure a good finish, the new carving is heavily sanded, and the rest of the frame is given a general sanding as well.

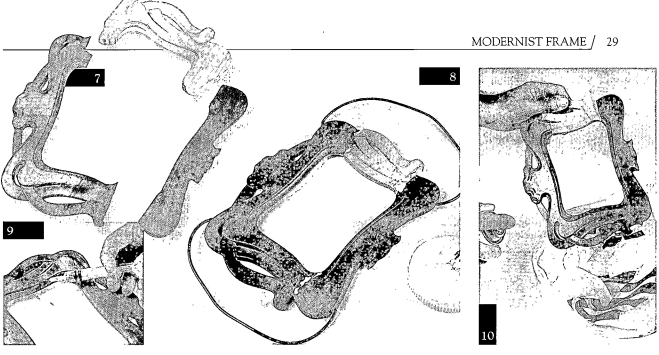

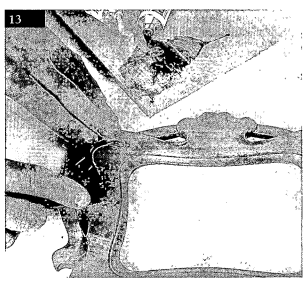

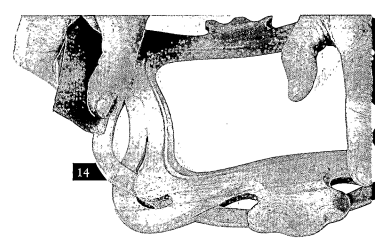

15. Then the color is evened out. This operation requires careful attention because only the new part is to be stained. To do this, it was necessary to mix the correct tone and to test the stain on another piece of wood.

16. Because the idea is to change the frame from a wall frame to a tabletop style, a piece of cherry wood is prepared for placement on the back side as a cover. The edges are cut with a circular saw so the new piece can be fit into the frame.

17. The edges are rounded with a plane on the outside of the cover, and then they are sanded vigorously with sandpaper.

18. The back support is designed with a similar style to that of the frame and the drawing is copied on a piece of wood with carbon paper.

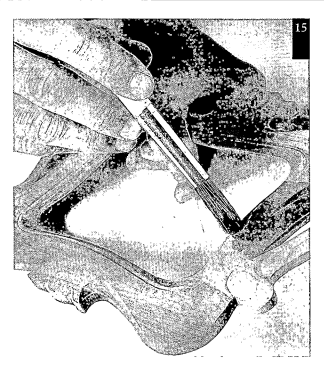

19. The outside of the frame's support is cut out with a jigsaw. The inside areas are pierced through so the saw can be inserted to do the cuts.

20. To finish shaping the support, it is held on the workbench with a clamp and the carving done with a gouge.

21. A final sanding is done on the entire surface of the support.

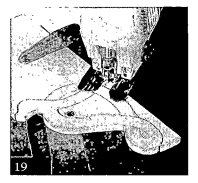

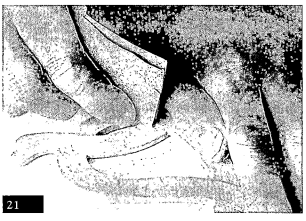

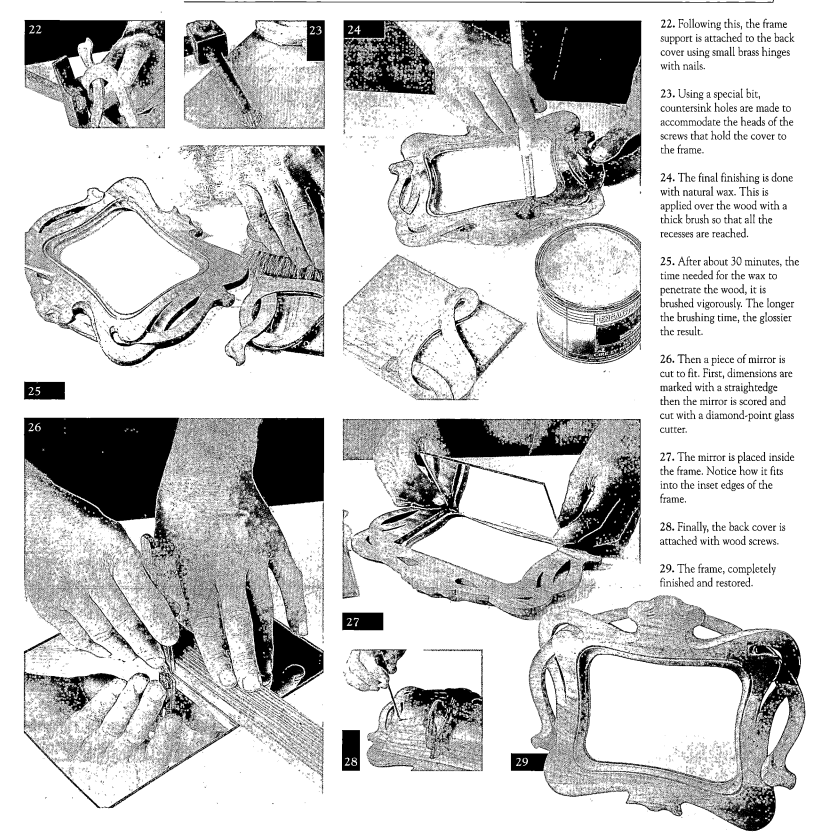

22. Following this, the frame support is attached to the back cover using small brass hinges with nails.

23. Using a special bit, countersink holes are made to accommodate the heads of the screws that hold the cover to the frame.

24. The final finishing is done with natural wax. This is applied over the wood with a thick brush so that all the recesses are reached.

25. After about 30 minutes, the time needed for the wax to penetrate the wood, it is brushed vigorously. The longer the brushing time, the glossier the result.

26. Then a piece of mirror is cut to fit. First, dimensions are marked with a straightedge then the mirror is scored and cut with a diamond-point glass cutter.

27. The mirror is placed inside the frame. Notice how it fits into the inset edges of the frame.

28. Finally, the back cover is attached with wood screws.

29. The frame, completely finished and restored.

BAROMETER BOX

Furniture pieces are not the only things that are restored; sometimes small decorative objects, which are only partly made of wood, are also restored.

In the next step-by-step exercise, a box made of oak wood housing a small meteorologic station with a barometer and a thermometer is restored.

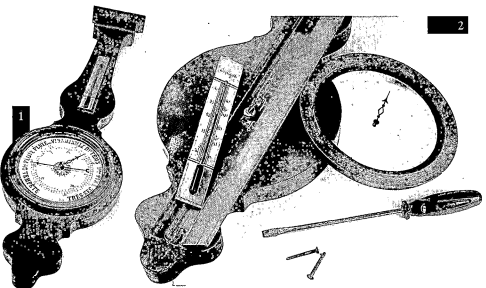

1. The wooden box that is going to be restored and the various components that are contained in it.

2. First, the wood box must be taken apart completely, removing all the pieces related to the barometer and the thermometer.

3. After evaluating the damage suffered with the passage of time and the infestation of wood-boring insects, an insecticide is injected to fill all the holes.

4. To guarantee that the insects are completely eliminated, the surface of the piece is sprayed with an insecticide, then the box is put into a plastic bag, sealed, and left for 10 to 15 days.

5. After this time has elapsed, the old varnish is removed. To do this, the entire box and the round frame are covered with stripping liquid, with a small brush, and are left for the product to work for a few minutes. Rubber gloves should be used.

6. When the varnish begins to crack, it is removed with the stripper, with a scraper blade. Notice the color of the raw wood.

7. The varnish and the stripper are removed from the round front frame by rubbing them with a few cotton strands soaked in solvent.

8. With the help of a small wooden spatula, filler of a color similar to oak is applied to all the holes that the wood-boring insects made. The desired tone is achieved by mixing fillers of different colors.

9. The same procedure is carried out on the back of the box and on the round frame.

10. The barometer's paper dial is cleaned using a rubber eraser, removing dirt and grime, while taking care not to damage the background.

11. Using white filler, the holes in the papers that the wood-boring insects made are filled.

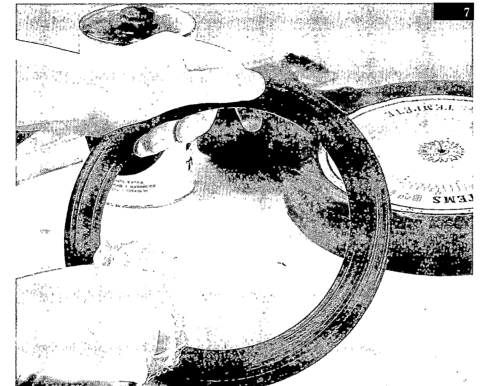

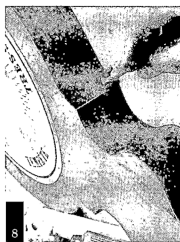

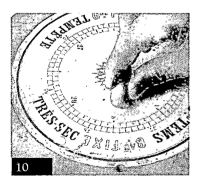

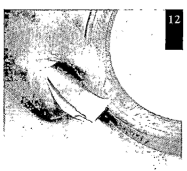

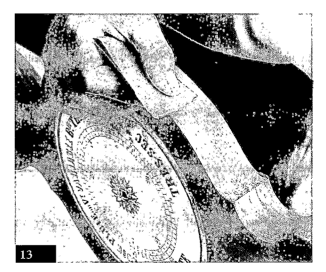

12. Once the barometer's background is cleaned, the round frame is sanded with medium-grit sandpaper, in order to remove traces of filler and leaving the surface completely smooth.

13. The side of the box, the barometer, and the remaining surfaces are also sanded.

14. When the box has been sanded, a sealer is applied as the base for the final finish, beginning with the round frame. Cotton rags are used to apply the product to the wood in thin layers.

15. The barometer box is sealed the same way, without getting any sealer on the barometer's paper dial.

16. Finally, varnish is applied with a finishing pad. Notice how the pad is able to reach all the corners in the molding.

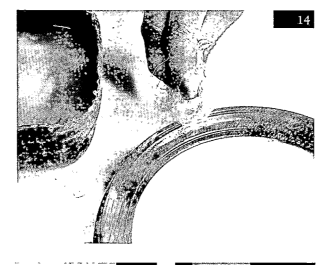

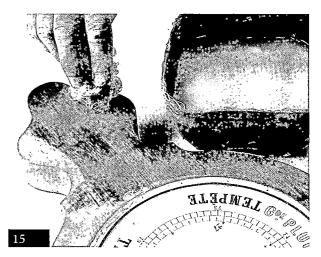

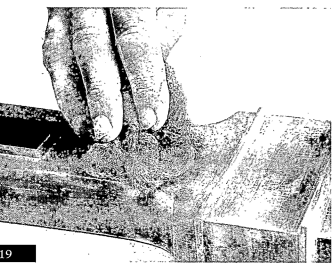

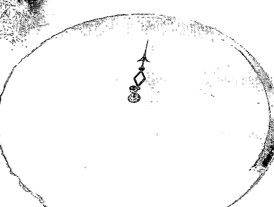

17. The same finish is applied to the box, covering all of the surfaces.

18. Then with a fine-grit sandpaper, the entire surface of the box is sanded.

19. Number 000 steel wool is used to polish the surface of the barometer and to achieve a flat and smooth surface.

20. The barometer's glass is washed with a window cleaner and wiped with a clean cotton cloth.

21. To clean the thermometer, the tube is taken off the backing that contains the measurements, and it is cleaned with a cotton rag dampened with a little alcohol.

22. The hands are cleaned with a metal cleaner and a cotton rag.

23. Then, the glass and the frame are put together and placed back onto the barometer box.

24. The frame is placed on the box with the holes in the barometer box lining up with those in the frame.

25. Then, the box is turned over and the two screws that hold the frame in place are tightened with a screwdriver.

26. The thermometer is placed inside the cutout area of the box made to hold it.

27. Finally, the only remaining task is to place the tubes of the barometer inside the box.

28. The barometer box completely restored and refinished.

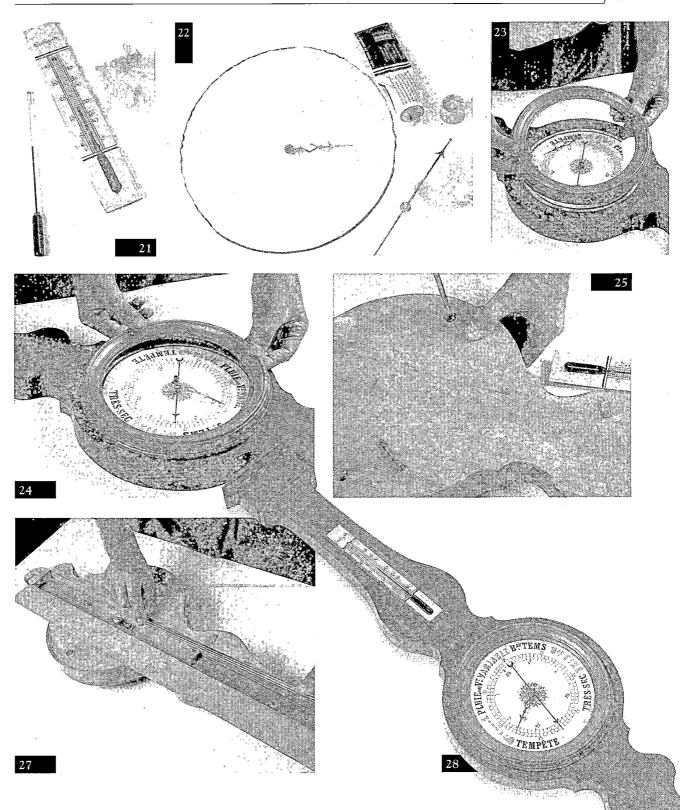

CHAIR WITH CANE WEBBING

When a piece of furniture or parts of it are brought in for repair, the restorer might be surprised to find that the piece had already been restored before. The following step-by-step exercise shows a chair that was repaired rather poorly some time ago. It is a chair whose front legs are slightly curved and joined to each other with stretchers. The seat was originally made of cane webbing. The back is open and some carvings can be seen on it. Because this chair is made of mahogany, there is no need to treat it for wood-boring insects because this wood is immune to them.

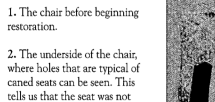

1. The chair before beginning restoration.

2. The underside of the chair, where holes that are typical of caned seats can be seen. This tells us that the seat was not originally made of wood. Also, notice that the crosspieces are broken.

3. The top of the chair back, like the rest of the chair, is dirty, broken, and missing material in the joints.

4. Also, notice that the rear side of the seat back has been reinforced with a metal angle brace.

5. To begin the restoration, the wood seat is removed by prying it off with a screwdriver. Pressure is applied upward so as not to damage the chair.

6. Then, with a small brush, the entire chair is covered with a commercial stripping product to remove the old varnish.

7. After several minutes have passed, the varnish softens and, with a scraper, the stripper is removed together with the old varnish.

8. The entire chair is cleaned with a cotton rag soaked in solvent, to eliminate traces of stripper that may still be on the piece.

9. The steel angle braces that are attached with screws to the back of the top of the chair are removed with a screwdriver.

10. Next, the joints of the chair are given some light taps using a hammer and a block of wood to disassemble the loose parts.

11. White glue is applied to the broken pieces of the sides of the seat, which are then clamped.

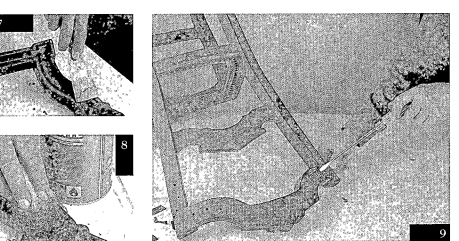

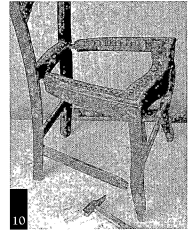

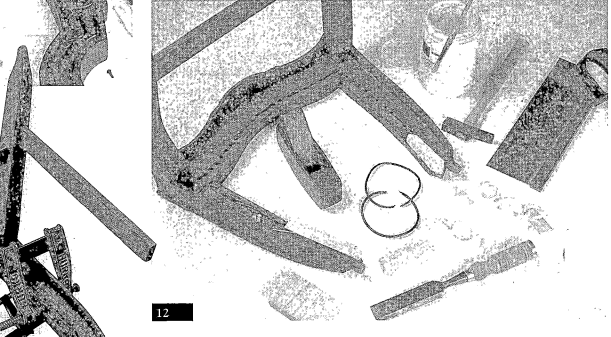

12. To add material, wood blocks are glued at the rear of the underside of the seat nails. Because these corners will not be visible, pine may be used.

13. Then, glue is applied to all the joints of the legs and the sides of the chairs.

14. With the help of a hammer and a wood block, the frame of the chair is assembled. The wood block is placed between the chair and the hammer to reduce the force of the hammer.

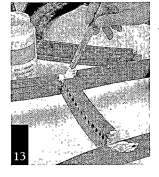

15. Clamps are placed to hold the seat assembly. Also, wood blocks are used with the clamps to avoid damage to the chair's wood at the points of pressure.

16. All the excess glue that oozes out of the joint is wiped off (before it dries) with a cotton rag soaked in water.

17. When the first phase of the restoration of the chair's seat is finished, the joints of the back's top crosspiece, which are broken, are fixed. With the tenon saw, a few cuts are made at the ends of the crosspiece to remove the damaged wood.

18. Two pieces of mahogany wood are cut and planed in the shape of a wedge.

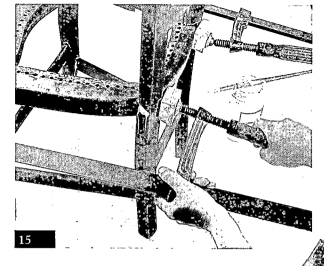

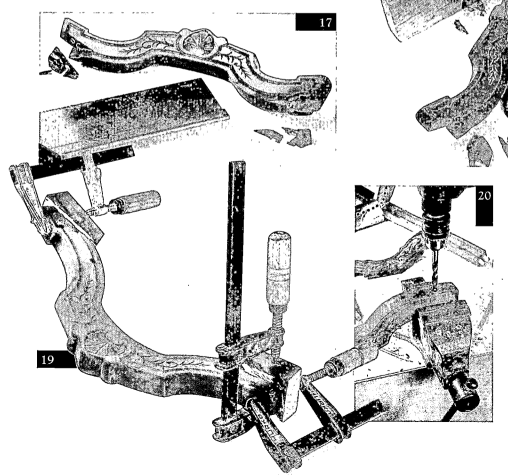

19. Next, the two mahogany pieces are bonded to the chair's crosspiece with white glue held in place with clamps.

20. When the glue is dry, the crosspiece is attached to the workbench, and the wood is shaped with a plane. Using a drill, holes are made for the insertion of some grooved dowels.

21. The dowels must be of the same thickness as the diameter of the holes. When the dowels have been put in place, glue is applied to the ends.

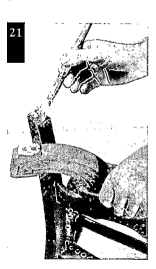

22. Then the chair back and the crosspiece are joined. The parts are helped into place with some taps with a hammer, making sure a block of wood is placed in between to avoid damaging the wood of the crosspiece.

23. All the pieces are held in place with a few large clamps. Before the excess glue dries, it is wiped off with a cotton rag or a cloth soaked in water.

24. When everything is dry, the clamps are removed and lines are traced to define the design of the carving on the chair's back. To do this, a pencil and a ruler or a straight piece of wood is used.

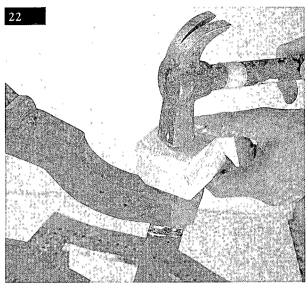

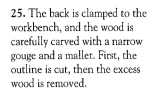

25. The back is clamped to the workbench, and the wood is carefully carved with a narrow gouge and a mallet. First, the outline is cut, then the excess wood is removed.

26. The holes left by the metal braces on the rear of the seat's back are covered with pieces of mahogany that have been cut to fit. They are bonded with white glue.

27. When the glue is dry, the strips are leveled with a rasp.

28. Once the repairs on the chair's back are finished, the restorer proceeds to the second part of the seat by preparing the holes of the caning with a drill bit of the same diameter as the existing holes. This will clean out the inside of those that may be clogged.

29. Then, any small imperfections are covered. This is done by applying stained filler of a color similar to mahogany with a chisel.

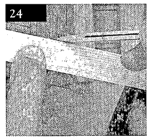

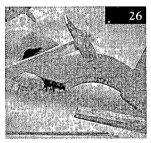

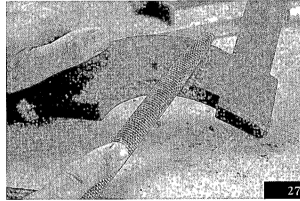

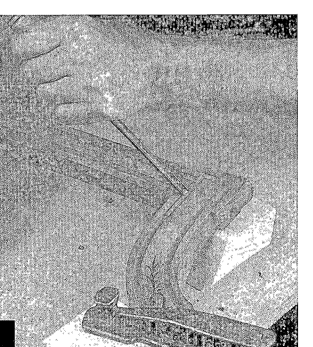

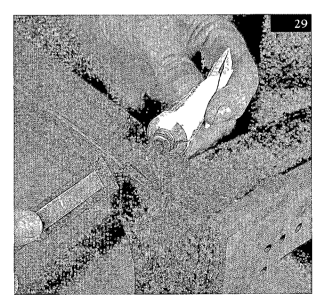

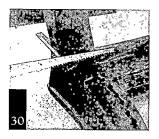

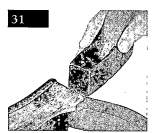

30. The space between the front leg and the seat's front crosspiece is filled by inserting a piece of wood of the same color that has been brushed with glue. The piece is trimmed with a keyhole saw.

31. The wood sticking out of the front is then planed smooth.

32. Finally, the entire chair is sanded to give it a smoother finish.

33. Then, fine sandpaper is used on the whole surface of the chair.

34. Next, a first layer of varnish is applied. In this case, filler is applied with a cotton rag, always rubbing in the direction of the grain of the wood.

35. When the varnish is dry, the entire surface is smoothed with a sanding block. Fine-grit sandpaper can also be used.

36. To achieve a higher degree of smoothness, the chair is polished with steel wool.

37. If the chair is to be glossy, wax is applied to it. For large surfaces, a cotton rag is used; for carved areas, a small brush is more comfortable and efficient.

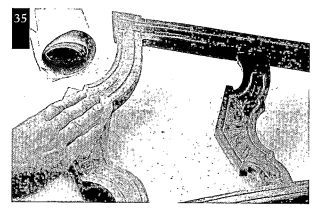

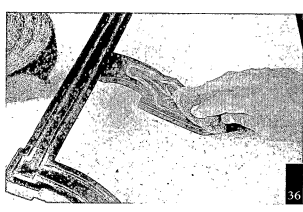

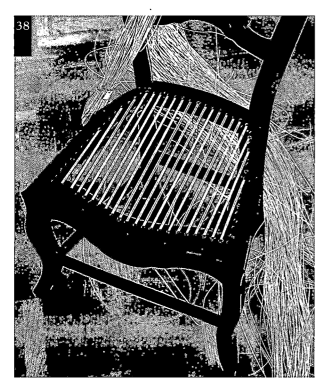

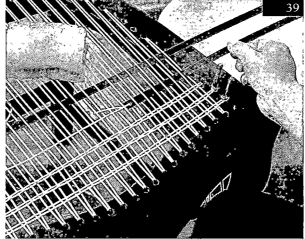

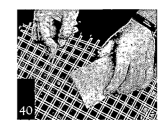

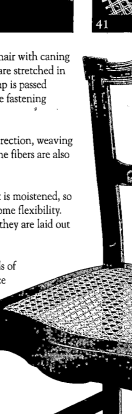

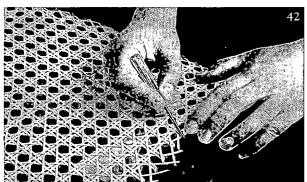

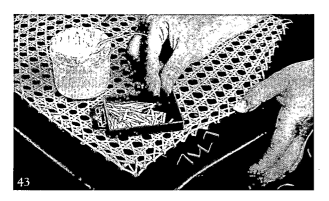

38. The one thing left to restore is the seat of the chair with caning made of a hemp fiber wicker. First, the hemp fibers are stretched in one direction through the holes. Each time the hemp is passed through a hole, white glue is applied to reinforce the fastening points.

39. Then, the fibers are stretched in the opposite direction, weaving them together with the help of a thin steel band. The fibers are also glued in these holes.

40. With a sponge and water, the surface of the seat is moistened, so the fibers that were rigid at the beginning acquire some flexibility. With a small screwdriver, the fibers are arranged so they are laid out properly and at the same distance.

41. Then the diagonal fibers are woven in. The ends of these fibers are trimmed with scissors, leaving a piece of about ¾ inch (2 cm) to attach them to the chair's holes.

42. The ends of the fibers woven in diagonally are tucked in the holes using a small screwdriver.

43. Finally, a piece of hemp is placed all around the seat. This is attached with small pieces of hemp bent in the middle, which are inserted in the holes with glue to guarantee they will stay in place.

44. The chair with cane webbing completely restored.

SIDE TABLE

Sometimes the entire piece of furniture has to be taken apart in order to restore it properly. The piece presented in the following exercise presents a challenge: It is a side table whose legs were attached with nails during its construction. This forces the restorer to take into account certain precautions while disassembling it and to use different methods than the original ones when putting the table back together.

1. The side table that is to be restored has four beechwood turned legs, joined to an elliptical top. The bottom part is reinforced with curved crosspieces. The glass top is also elliptical.

2. First, a general evaluation of the damage is made. The wood has suffered insect infestation, and it also suffers from aging of the varnish and the paint on all of the parts.

3. The edge of the tabletop is broken in places. In this case, the best solution is to remove them completely and to bond them properly once they have been repaired.

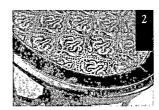

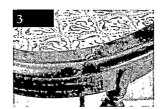

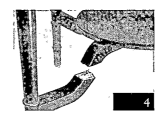

4. The crosspieces that join the legs with the table's bottom shelf are broken or have come unglued.

5. Now, the entire table is taken apart. First, the glass piece and the backing board that serves as a support must be removed. The nails that join the round piece to the table are pulled out with pincers.

6. The board is removed along with the decorative fabric of the tabletop.

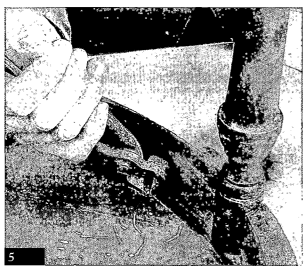

7. Then, the decorative parts that are attached with nails to the tops of the legs are carefully removed with a screwdriver.

8. The small shelf at the bottom of the table is also removed with the same care.

9. Next, with a screwdriver or another pointed tool, the inside of the round frame is cleaned, removing all the sawdust and, if possible, any wood-boring insects that may have settled there.

10. To finish with the disassembly of the table, the legs are removed. Using the hand or a screwdriver as a lever is sufficient, because the legs are joined with nails.

11. Then, all the pieces of the table are stripped. The stripping gel is applied with a brush, beginning with the legs.

12. The stripper is removed together with the damaged varnish by rubbing the piece with a cotton rag soaked in solvent. Gloves are recommended for this step.

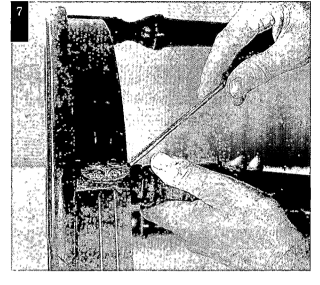

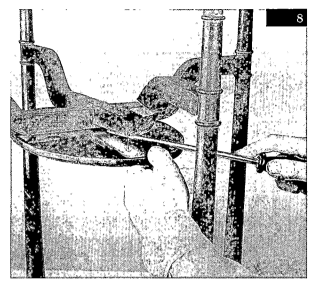

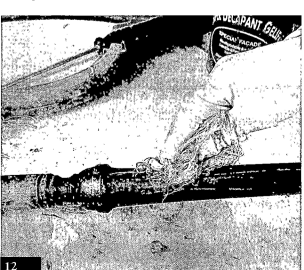

13. When wood has been infested by insects, they must be completely eliminated. An insecticide is injected in all the holes to accomplish this.

14. All the pieces that have been treated with insecticide are put into a plastic bag, which is closed tightly. The pieces are left in the bag for 24 hours and the procedure is repeated in 15 days.

15. After cleaning and treating the pieces, the broken ones are repaired. The restorer begins with the lower crosspiece, gluing the broken pieces and holding them in place with spring clamps or screws, if any other way of exerting pressure is not possible.

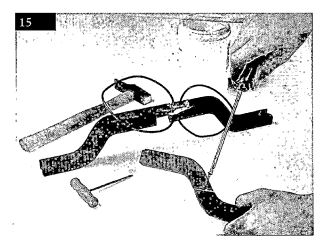

16. The oval frame of the table-top, which is broken, is glued on both sides with white glue.

17. Both parts are joined with a screw that will hold them in place.

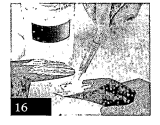
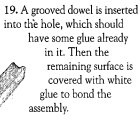

18. The ends of the two halves of the oval must be joined with wood dowels. To do this, the part is clamped to the workbench and the wood bored with a drill bit of about ⁵⁄₁₆ inches (8 mm) in diameter, for the insertion of a dowel.

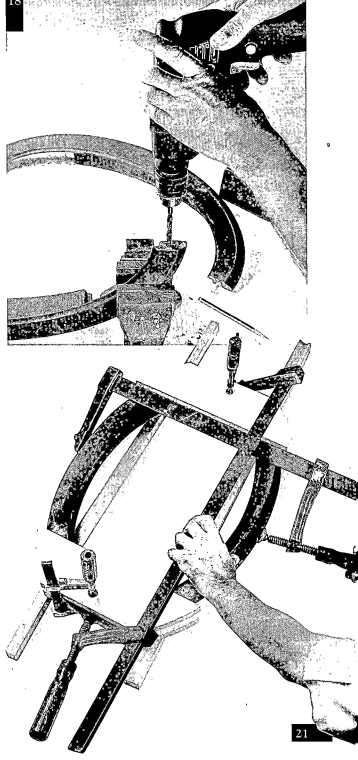

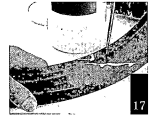

19. A grooved dowel is inserted into the hole, which should have some glue already in it. Then the remaining surface is covered with white glue to bond the assembly.

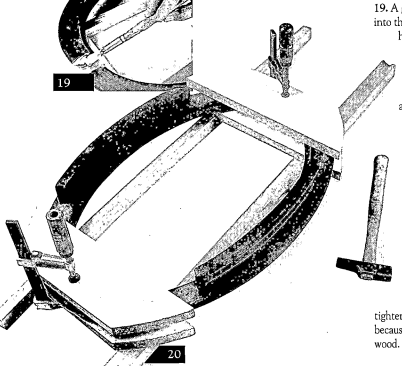

20. To guarantee a good bond, small clamps are first placed on both ends, with boards that will help spread the pressure evenly.

21. Next, two additional larger clamps are placed perpendicularly one next to the other. Avoid tightening them too much because they could damage the wood.

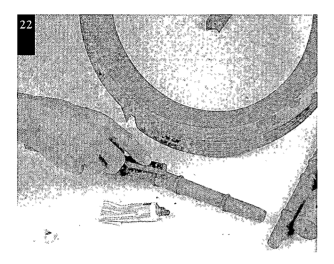

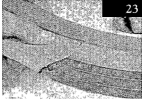

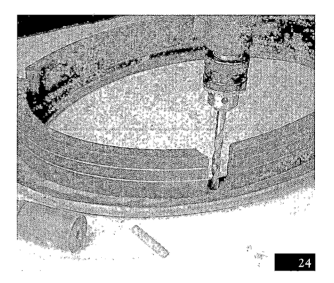

22. Then, all the insect holes and small imperfections are covered with filler. This is done with a chisel.

23. When the filler is dry, the entire frame is sanded with a medium-grit sandpaper.

24. To join the legs to the round table frame assembly, holes are bored with a drill in the top end of the legs and also on the underside of the round frame. Glued wood dowels are inserted in the holes of the legs.

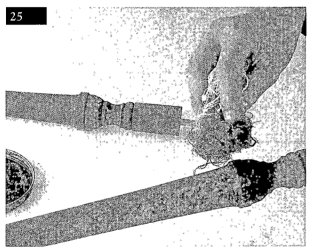

25. Before proceeding with the assembly, a slightly red stain is applied to the legs with a cotton rag or cheesecloth.

26. Next, the legs are varnished, applying the product with a cheesecloth.

27. Then, the frame of the tabletop is varnished the same way, along with the remaining table parts.

28. When the varnish dries, it is rubbed with a sanding sponge, which is specially made for this purpose, or with sandpaper. This illustration depicts the sanding of the round frame, but the entire table is done the same way.

29. The next step consists of polishing the entire piece with a steel wool pad, to achieve a higher degree of smoothness.

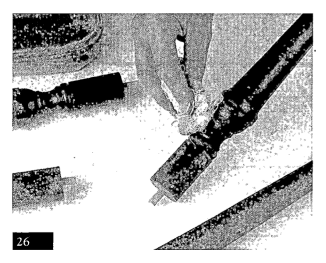

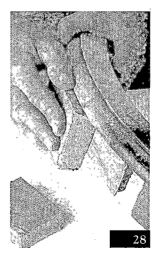

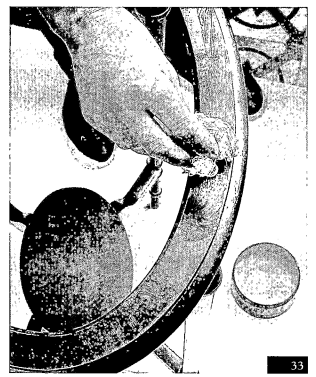

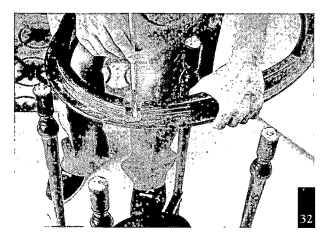

30. Next, the legs can be assembled. They are held together with curved cross-pieces, joined with screws.

31. To conceal the screws, a mixture of colored waxes has been prepared, forming a paste that is applied with a small wooden spatula over the tops of the screws.

32. The legs and the oval frame are brushed with glue, also applying glue to the wood dowels and joining all of the parts together.

33. For the final finish of the table, wax is applied, rubbing vigorously to obtain the desired glossy smooth appearance.

34. The decorative fabric of the tabletop is cleaned by rubbing trichlorethylene on it with a brush. This step is repeated as many times as needed, depending on how dirty the fabric is.

35. The glass top that protects the fabric is cleaned with a window cleaner applied with cheesecloth.

36. The hardware is cleaned with a metal cleaner. The restorer spreads the paste over the metal and rubs it until the natural gloss is achieved.

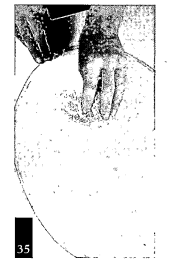

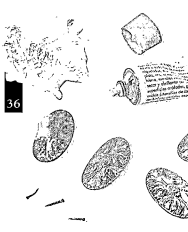

37. In order to preserve the glossy finish and prevent the hardware piece from oxidizing, a coat of lacquer is applied with a small brush.

38. The decorative hardware is installed with small nails, being careful not to strike the table or metal with the hammer.

39. Next, the glass piece is put in place from under the table, resting it on the ledge.

40. The cleaned, restored fabric is placed over the glass.

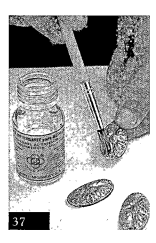

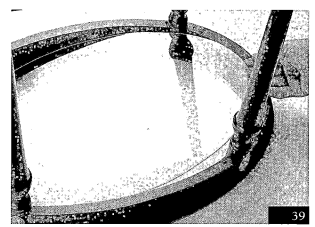

41. After the fabric, the backing board is put in place to hold the assembly together. The board is attached to the table with small nails.

42. The piece must be dusted and newly waxed before the project can be considered finished. Then, the entire surface is buffed with cheese-cloth to make it shine.

43. The side table, after being completely restored and finished.

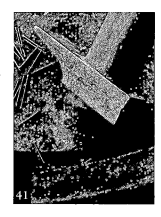

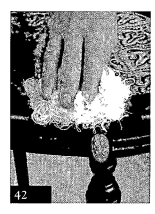

BUREAU

*T*he bureau piece that will be restored is a handcrafted antique consisting of four frontal drawers and a drop front that conceals a fifth drawer. The structure is made of pinewood, veneered with walnut, and the moldings and frontal carvings are solid walnut. The inside of the bureau is veneered with a lighter wood, such as maple. And to top it all off, there is a piece of white marble.

1. As with every restoration, the job begins by going over the imperfections of the piece. This is a bureau whose drop-front lid in front has come off.

2. A typical occurrence with many pieces of furniture is the loss of small parts. In this case, a small piece of molding is missing.

3. One of the first steps consists of making the piece as light as possible for the restoration. To do this, the top marble piece is removed, storing it in a safe place to prevent any breakage.

4. Next, the drawers are taken out, and the piece of furniture is visually inspected.

5. The bottom part has broken or missing veneer pieces. It also has holes made in the wood by wood-boring insects.

6. Another problem is that the side veneer pieces are coming unglued, perhaps caused by humidity that this piece may have been exposed to during its long life. Also, some veneer loss is observed on the frame.

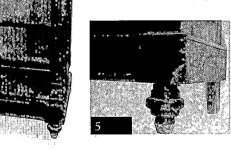

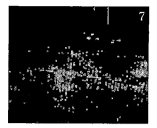

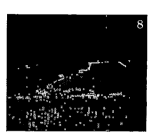

7. At the rear, infestation by wood-boring insects is apparent on the backboards. This is a symptom of the piece being dirty and exposed to humidity.

8. There are some wood pieces on the back of the piece of furniture that, because of insect infestation, must be replaced.

9. Once the evaluation is completed, restoration begins by injecting insecticide with a syringe. This procedure will eliminate the insects that may still be living in the wood.

10. Next, the piece is cleaned with a cotton rag soaked in alcohol. The finish on this piece is shellac, and alcohol is an excellent solvent for this varnish.

11. One of the front legs, which is a turned piece, has broken off the furniture because of the wood-boring insects.

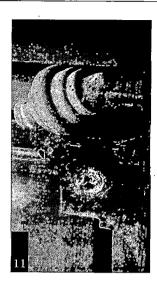

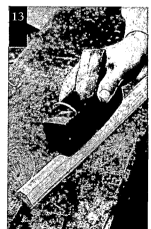

12. To repair it, the leg is clamped to the workbench, and its top is drilled with a bit about ½ inch (13 mm) in diameter.

13. To secure the leg firmly to the underside of the body, a wood dowel is made with the same diameter as the hole bored in the leg; the edges are beveled with a plane.

14. The dowel is tapped into the hole of the leg with a hammer.

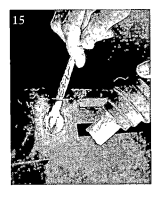

15. To complete the joint, the wood dowel is cut to the size of the hole, and white glue is applied to it to ensure a good bond.

16. Meanwhile, the rabbit skin glue is prepared. To do this, the glue is mixed with water in a small pot and heated in a double boiler.

17. Then, a few small cuts are made with a chisel on the side veneer, to make the process of applying glue easier. Notice how the chisel is run along the molding.

18. When the glue is ready, it is applied to the veneer with a small brush. To make the job easier, the veneer is lifted with a scraping blade.

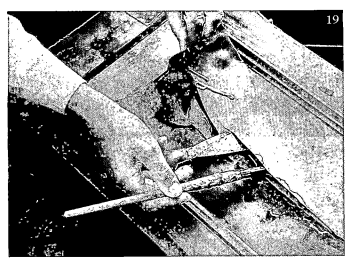

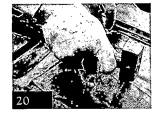

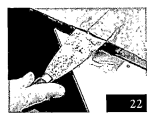

19. With the veneer lifted up, the glue can be evenly spread.

20. Pressure is applied to the veneer with the veneering hammer to make sure it is well adhered.

21. To reinforce the bond, uniform pressure is applied with clamps, for about two hours.

22. The veneer of the drop front, which had come unglued, is reattached by applying glue with a scraping blade.

23. Pressure is applied with a clamp. To help distribute the force evenly, a melamine-covered board is used, which will help prevent the wood from sticking.

24. Small cuts are made in the blisters with a chisel.

25. Next, glue is inserted in the cuts with a thin and pointed tool, pressing it later to guarantee the complete adherence of the veneer to the base.

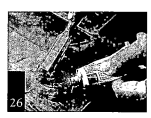

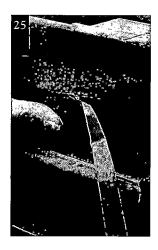

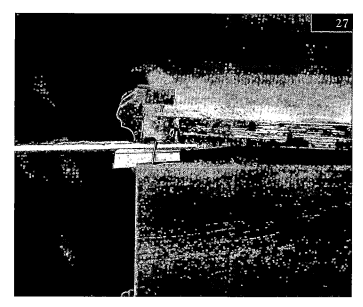

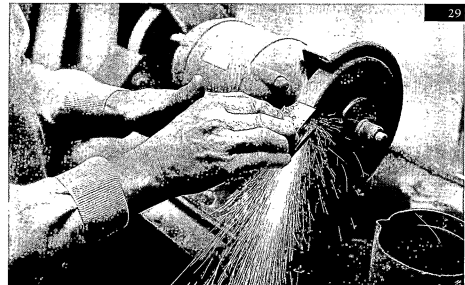

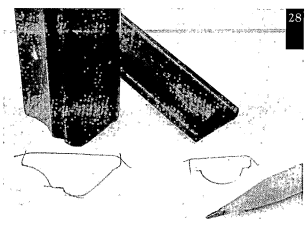

26. The imperfections that the wood-boring insects caused and the small blemishes are repaired with filler. The filler should have a tone as close as possible to that of the wood.

27. The top part of the furniture piece is also removed, using a screwdriver as a lever. A piece of wood is placed in between to avoid damage to the piece of furniture from the prying.

28. When the moldings are damaged or get lost, one must be removed to be used as a model to copy the profile.

29. With a grinding machine, a steel blank is shaped to make a blade that will serve to cut the moldings.

30. The form of the future cutting blade will be finished by sanding it with a round file.

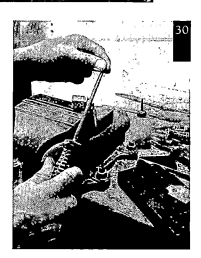

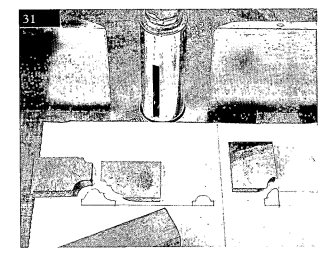

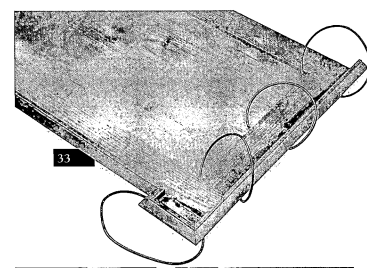

31. Notice how the shapes of the molding copied on paper coincide with the cutting blades.

32. The cutting blades are placed in a shaper. When the blades rotate at high speed, the wood may be passed through several times to make the molding.

33. Once the length of molding has been cut, it is bonded to the structure with white glue, and it is held with spring clamps.

34. Next, veneer is applied to the sides with glue, cutting the excess material with a chisel.

35. A scraping blade is used to polish the veneer. This tool must always go in the direction of the wood grain.

36. When the entire surface has been scraped, it is sanded with sandpaper wrapped around a sanding block, which will help make the task easier.

37. The old veneer that is still on the piece is also scraped with a scraping blade. This must be done carefully so as not to damage the veneer.

38. Also, the original molding must be rid of dried out glue. To do this, work the surface with the chisel by holding it with the right hand and scraping across the wood.

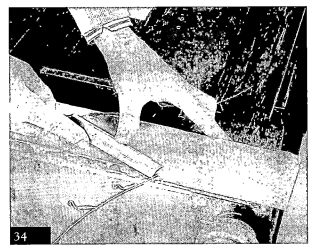

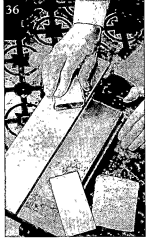

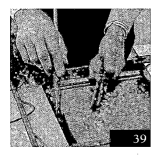

39. All the molding and remaining pieces are bonded with rabbit skin glue and held in place with spring clamps.

40. A piece of wood, the same size as the leg, is glued on the back leg that was broken.

41. A piece of a horizontal brace on the back of the bureau is cut off and replaced with another one made of new wood, thus eliminating a part of the furniture piece that was very damaged by wood-boring insects. Notice how the piece to be replaced is being marked.

42. A crosscut is made on the horizontal wood brace using a tenon saw.

43. What is left of the damaged wood is removed with a chisel and a hammer, up to the previously made cut.

44. Rabbit skin glue is applied on the piece of wood, and it is added to the brace. Pressure is applied with spring clamps, and a length of wood and two clamps are used to apply pressure in the center of the piece.

45. When the glue is dry, the entire piece is sanded with medium-grit sandpaper, in the same direction as the grain of the wood.

46. The same procedure is re-peated on each of the moldings, sanding all the corners and edges.

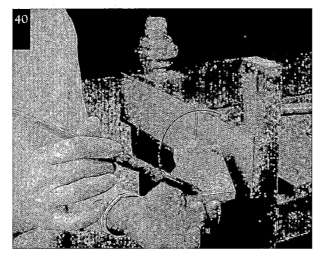

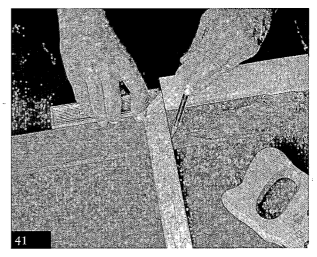

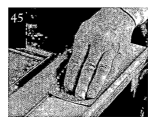

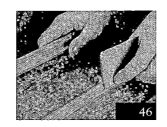

47. All the new pieces are stained in order to match the color of the bureau; a commercial stain is used for this, applied with a cotton rag.

48. When the stain is dry, varnish can be applied over the entire surface of the piece with cheesecloth, which will allow the varnish to reach all the corners.

49. For the final finish, shellac is applied with a rubbing pad. This will guarantee that the surfaces will end up perfectly smooth and even.

50. A small paintbrush is used to varnish the carvings on the front.

51. Before replacing the drop front lid, small repairs must be made on the interior veneer. Small pieces of veneer are brushed with glue and applied to the missing areas, and the edges are trimmed with a chisel.

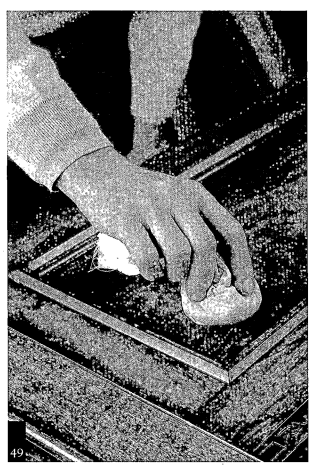

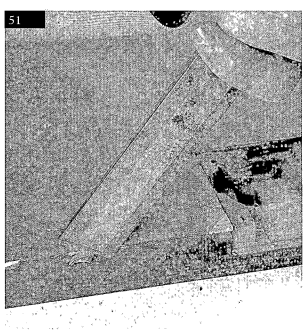

52. These small pieces must also be stained so that the color will match the rest of the drop front.

53. Now, all that is left to do is touching up. First, a special two-part epoxy adhesive is prepared.

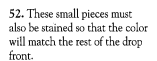

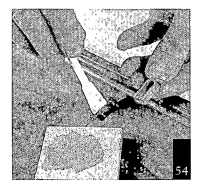

54. This glue is used to bond the keyhole to the wood drop front. The glue is applied with a plastic spatula because of its high toxicity.

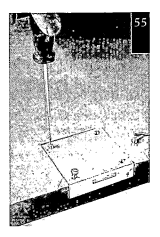

55. Next, the lock is attached with screws. In many instances, it is necessary to adjust the new lock to fit the wood.

56. The polishing and the buffing of the marble piece are also considered part of the finishing step. To polish the marble, a piece of pumice is dampened and rubbed over the marble surface while exerting a light pressure.

57. To make it shine, cheesecloth is dipped in furniture wax and rubbed over the surface of the marble; then the surface is buffed with a dry cloth until the desired shine is achieved.

58. The clean and polished marble is set back into place.

59 and 60. The bureau completely restored, inside and out.

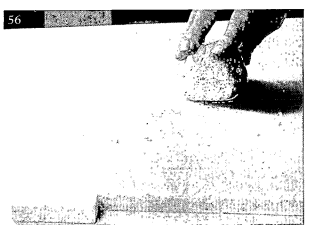

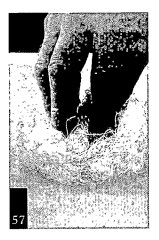

CHEST OF DRAWERS

*T*he piece of furniture that is going to be restored is a dresser without a definite style. Its construction dates back to about 1860. It is made of different types of woods; the interior structure is pine, and the top and the front decorations are solid mahogany. The sides and the drawers are made of pine veneered with mahogany and strips of boxwood. The drawer bottoms are made of poplar.

The dresser is of great interest because it is one of the most commonly restored furniture pieces.

In order to understand all the processes, the steps required to restore the piece have been strictly followed. First, the extent of the damage is evaluated, and then the tasks—such as cleaning, repairs, additions, replacements, sanding, and finishes—that are needed by the piece of furniture itself and some of the decorative pieces—such as veneer, carvings, and marquetry—are planned.

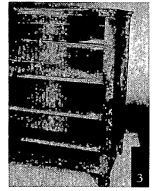

1. The condition of the piece of furniture when it arrived at the workshop.

2. The top of the dresser is broken on one side and pieces of veneer have come loose in different areas of the piece.

3. The wood of the inside of the piece shows heavy wear and the top drawer support is broken.

4. The bottoms of the drawers are broken and the guides are worn out.

5. There is general damage around the keyholes and locks, and there is grime on the veneer and marquetry.

6. The top and the back of the dresser have scratches, darkened areas, stains, and grime.

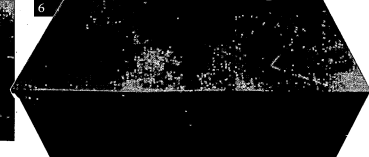

7. To begin the restoration, the small parts of the piece are removed and restored—in this case, the carved posts.

8. Then, the posts are cleaned: A commercial stripper is applied to them with a small brush.

9. The outermost parts of the column are cleaned by wiping them with cheesecloth soaked in solvent.

10. Using a brush with plastic bristles, the remnants of varnish are eliminated from hard to reach places.

11. To clean the fronts of the drawers, they must be soaked with a commercial stripper, which is applied with a wide brush.

12. The varnish and the stripper are removed at the same time with a spatula.

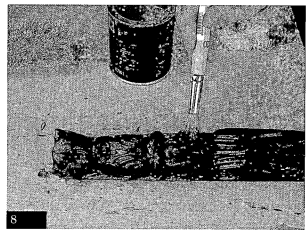

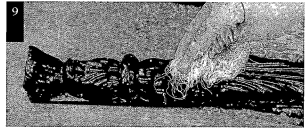

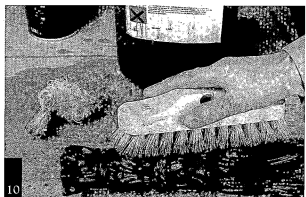

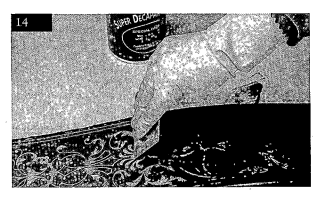

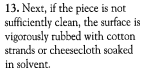

13. Next, if the piece is not sufficiently clean, the surface is vigorously rubbed with cotton strands or cheesecloth soaked in solvent.

14. The surface must be scraped with a scraping blade to be thoroughly cleaned.

15. The furniture top is cleaned the same way, stripping and scraping off the old varnish.

16. Then with a scraping blade, the surface is scraped for deeper cleaning.

17. The piece of furniture with the old varnish removed.

18. When repairing the drawer bottoms, the parts are marked and numbered before they are removed.

19. The bottoms are removed, using a screwdriver as a lever.

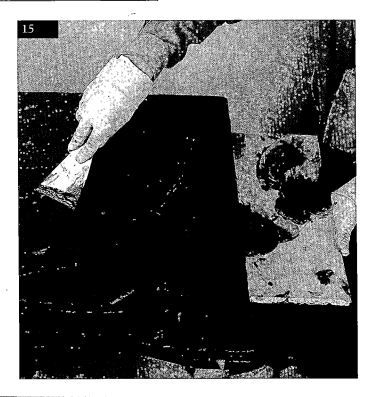

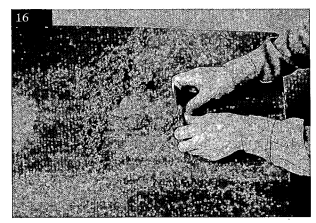

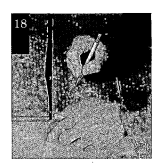

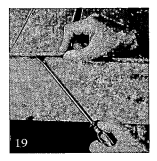

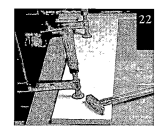

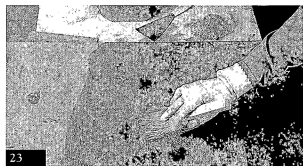

20. The parts of the drawer bottoms are arranged on a board, which is laid across two sawhorses. Their repair requires the addition of a piece.

21. White glue is applied with a small brush.

22. The parts are bonded together and held in place with the appropriate clamps and wedges.

23. The drawer bottoms are also dirty and they must be cleaned with a solution of ammonia and water.

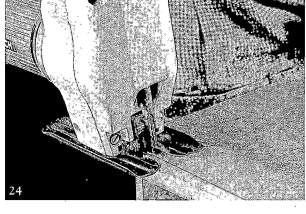

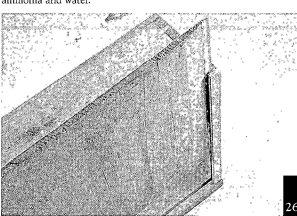

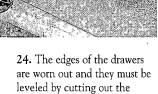

24. The edges of the drawers are worn out and they must be leveled by cutting out the damaged area.

25. Next, a strip of wood is glued on and held in place with spring clamps.

26. The cleaned and repaired bottom boards are placed back in the drawers.

27. Then the bottom is attached to the drawer with nails.

28. The support of the top drawer is repaired by applying white glue to the broken part.

29. The glued piece is held in place with a clamp.

30. We then proceed to repair the fronts of the drawers. First, patterns are made of the damaged area around the keyhole.

31. The damaged areas are removed from the front with a chisel.

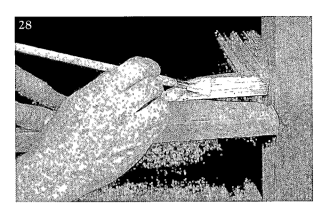

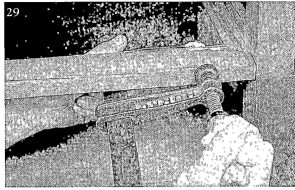

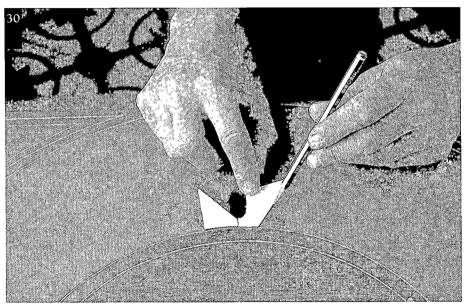

32. After the damaged area is cut away, the pieces made from the patterns are glued on.

33. The replaced parts are made of a ³⁄₁₆-inch (5 mm) thick veneer that was previously prepared.

34. Next, the other damaged areas are removed from the drawer fronts using a chisel.

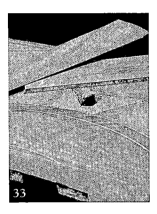

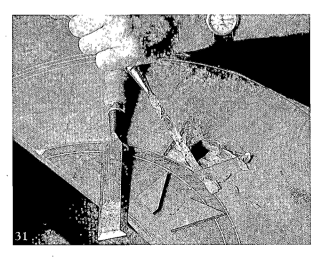

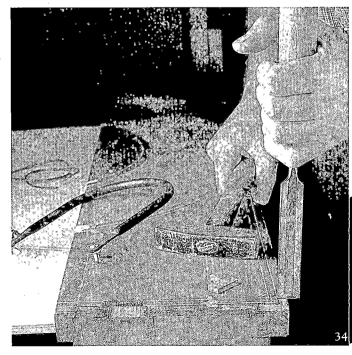

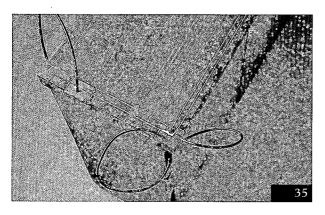

35. The small pieces are glued on and held in place with spring clamps.

36. Then, the strips of boxwood veneer are inserted in the grooves and marked. They are removed, glued, and inserted again.

37. To repair the top of the dresser, the wood of the damaged area is eliminated with a rabbet plane.

38. A piece of mahogany is bonded to the dresser and held in place with clamps.

39. The added piece is shaped with a jigsaw.

40. The edges of the added part are rounded with a rasp and shaped to match the original form of the piece of furniture.

41. Finally, the part is sanded to make it blend with the chest of drawers.

42. To replace the damaged veneer, the small pieces that will be inserted in the broken areas are marked.

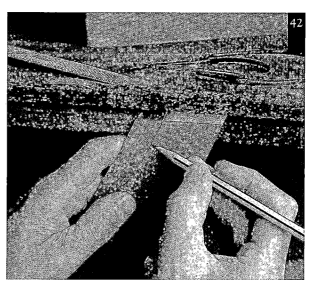

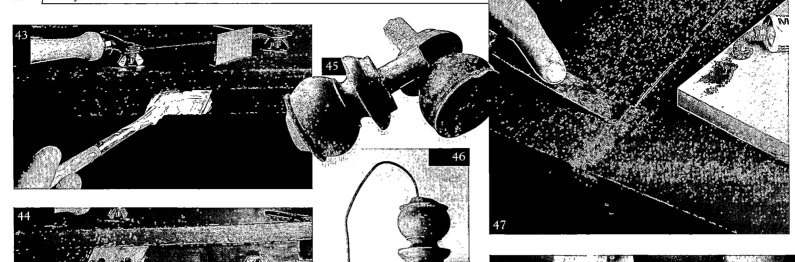

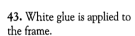

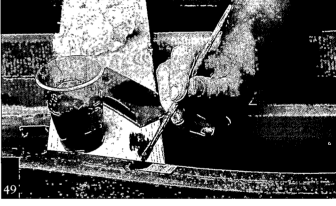

43. White glue is applied to the frame.

44. The added pieces are held in place with spring clamps.

45. The feet of the dresser are also quite worn and have some broken areas.

46. To repair them, glue is applied to the pieces and they are put back in place, making sure that the damaged areas face the back of the piece of furniture.

47. The small cracks in the furniture are restored with fillers.

48. Once the entire piece is restored, it is sanded.

49. The color of the newly added pieces is matched to the old with aniline dyes.

50. Also, the tones of all the parts that are lighter in color with respect to the overall piece must also be matched to the darker tones.

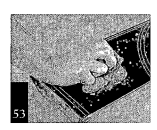

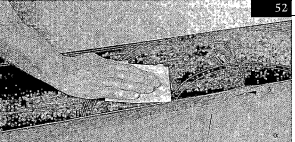

51. The piece is varnished with cotton strands or cheesecloth.

52. When the varnish is dry, it is sanded with a very-fine-grit sandpaper.

53. The surface is then buffed with 000 steel wool, to achieve a smoother finish.

54. Beeswax is applied with a cloth or cotton strands.

55. The keyholes for the locks are attached with epoxy glue.

56. The keyholes and keys after attachment to the drawers.

57. The restored chest of drawers.

GLOSSARY

Adhesive tape. Paper or plastic tape with glue that adheres by simple contact.

Aniline. Synthetic pigment used for staining wood or coloring fillers.

Bleach (to). To lighten the wood's color by using certain chemicals.

Brush. A flat, wide brush or a fine artist's paintbrush is used to spread stain or varnish on wood.

Bubble. Small area of veneer that has come unglued causing it to warp.

Buff (to). To eliminate the wood's raised grain to make the natural grain shinier.

Buffing pad. Cheesecloth or fibers wrapped in a cloth that is used to apply shellac or varnish to wood in very fine coats.

Carpenter's glue. White glue.

Caustic soda. A chemical soluble in water and highly corrosive, used for removing paint and varnish from the wood.

Contact cement. A type of adhesive most commonly used to glue melamine and veneer.

Countersink. Technique for boring the wood to insert the top of a screw until it is level with the wood or a little below the surface.

Dowel. Small cylindrical wood piece that is used to hold and reinforce joints.

End grain. Surface produced after sawing wood perpendicularly to the fibers.

Finish. The last treatment that is applied to a restored wood object of a piece of furniture.

Handled scraper. A steel tool with sharp edges, and sometimes teeth, used to clean surfaces and to eliminate old paint. It is also used to spread glue evenly over a flat surface.

Hygroscopic. Describes a material whose moisture content tends to stay the same as the humidity of its surroundings.

Join (to). To put two pieces together using the mortise and tenon method.

Molding. Element with uniform relief and profile used as decoration.

Mortise. Rectangular hole made in the wood for joining with a tenon.

Rabbit skin glue. An adhesive made from the hide and bones of the animal. In the past, it was often used for bonding pieces of wood. Nowadays, it is not used very much, except for gluing veneer. It is available in the form of flakes or fine granules, which must be dissolved in hot water in a double boiler.

Sanding. The action of rubbing a surface with sandpaper to make it smooth.

Scraping. Method of stripping or polishing solid wood that is shaped or that is in a bad state of repair by using scrapers or scraping blades.

Shellac. Resin available in flakes, made from insects that live in the wood. It comes in various colors. It is soluble in alcohol and in water.

Stain (to). To color the wood without covering the pattern of the grain.

Strip (to). To remove varnish or paint layers that cover the wood.

Tenon. The end of a piece of wood made thinner than the rest, which allows it to be inserted and fixed in a matching hole in another piece of wood.

Turpentine. Substance obtained from pine and other conifers, used to make varnish.

Varnish. A solution of gum or resin in a solvent that, when applied on a surface, dries and forms a coating that is more or less glossy, transparent, and waterproof.

Veneer. A very fine sheet of wood that is applied as a covering layer.

Veneered. A piece of wood that is covered with veneer.

Wax. An animal or vegetable substance that is used as a finishing coat on wood surfaces.

White glue. A polyvinyl acetate adhesive, also known as carpenter's glue. It is one of the least expensive and easiest adhesives to use. It is excellent for all-purpose use, and it is not toxic.

Wood-boring insect. An insect that consumes wood.